SHARKS
Myth and Reality

Gaetano Cafiero

Maddalena Jahoda

THOMASSON-GRANT
CHARLOTTESVILLE, VIRGINIA

SHARKS
Myth and Reality

Text
Gaetano Cafiero
Maddalena Jahoda

Editorial Director
Valeria Manferto

Design
Patrizia Balocco

Illustrations
Monica Falcone

Translated by
Antony Shugaar

Scientific consultant, English edition:
Marcelo R. de Carvalho,
Department of Ichthyology,
American Museum
of Natural History

FACING *The great white shark is the most feared shark in the world; its reputation as a killer has been heightened by a series of popular movies.*

2-3 *The mysterious mass gatherings of hammerhead sharks constitute one of the most exciting and unsettling spectacles the underwater world has to offer. Pictured here is a group of* Sphyrna lewini *swimming off the coasts of the Galápagos Islands.*

4-5 *The sand tiger shark* (Carcharias taurus) *often swims along with its mouth open, revealing the menacing "ragged" teeth with which it devours small prey.*

6-7 *A great blue shark benefits from huge gatherings of squid during their mating season.*

10-11 *Divers in Australia observe great white sharks* (Carcharodon carcharias) *from a special protective cage.*

Published in 1994 by
Thomasson-Grant, Inc.
World Copyright © 1994
Edizioni White Star, Via
Candido Sassone 22/24
13100, Vercelli, Italy

All rights reserved.
This book, or any portions
thereof, may not be
reproduced in any form
without written permission
from the publisher.

Inquiries should be
directed to:
Thomasson-Grant, Inc.
One Morton Drive
Suite 500
Charlottesville, Virginia,
22903-6806

Photography credited
on page 144.
Printed in February 1994
by Typolithographic
Canale, Torino. Fotolito
La Cromografica Ghemme
(Novara)

99 98 97 96 95 94 5 4 3 2 1

Library of Congress
Cataloging-in-Publication
Data on page 144.

Contents

Preface

Sharks have always held a special place in the collective imagination of humanity. Subjects of fantastic myths and legends, objects of worship, symbols of ancient civilizations, and even "stars" on the silver screen, they have been a source of fear and fascination for centuries. But what we know today about the behavior of sharks makes us less wary of them and helps us to protect them from exploitation and senseless slaughter. Sharks provide a remarkably wide range of products, from vitamin-rich oils, squalene, and anticoagulants to leather. Today we are less concerned with how to avoid falling prey to sharks and more concerned with how to best utilize them as valuable marine resources.

We are still learning about them, however, and questions about sharks have no easy answers, so great is the variety of species, sizes, habits, and habitats. The anatomical differences between cartilaginous fish (sharks, rays, and chimaeras) and bony fish are so great that it is impossible to class them together. The former, members of the class Chondrichthyes, all have cartilaginous skeletons, which are less complex than true bony skeletons.

The first part of this book, illustrated with spectacular color photographs, covers the many centuries of interaction between humans and sharks and is enriched by diver and author Gaetano Cafiero's firsthand accounts of encounters with sharks—in the Mediterranean Sea and in the great open expanses of the oceans, from the Indian Ocean to the corals of the Great Barrier Reef of Australia. The second section of the book approaches the subject from a more scientific point of view; the text, written by Maddalena Jahoda, is accompanied by drawings, charts, and maps rendered by Monica Falcone.

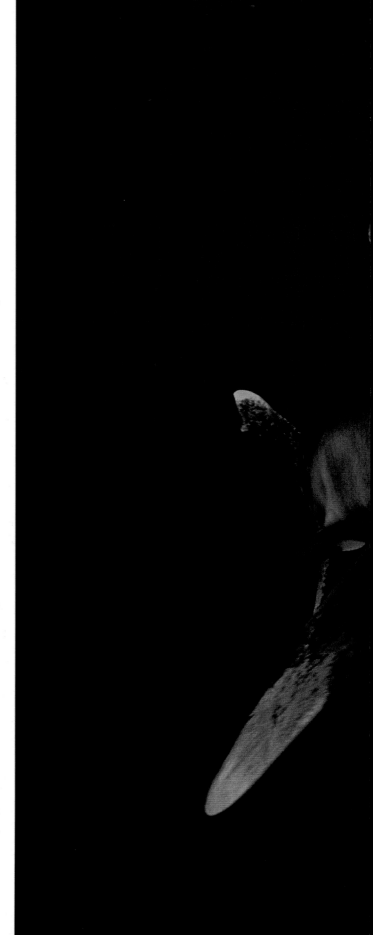

RIGHT *The oceanic white tip shark* (Carcharhinus maou), *a requiem shark, is common throughout the tropical and warm-to-temperate seas of the world. It can be recognized by its long, rounded pectoral fins; the first dorsal fin is round and broad with a light tip. These sharks usually live in the open seas, far from the continental masses, though in a few cases they have been known to come close enough to the coasts to be found in shallow waters.*

This shark is considered to be potentially dangerous and has been known to attack humans in a number of cases. The average white tip shark is just under ten feet long. Pilot fish, such as those swimming around this shark, tend to swim with sharks and rays to take advantage of floating scraps of food and also to seek the protection of the fearsome predator that serves as their "chaperone." In ancient times it was believed that pilot fish could guide sharks toward the areas richest in food.

14-15 *The whale shark* (Rhincodon typus) *is the largest fish known to science; its mouth may be as much as six-and-a-half feet across.*

16-17 *The white-tip reef shark* (Triaenodon obesus) *is active chiefly at night. By day it tends to remain hidden in its grotto.*

18-19 Etmopterus spinax *is a small shark (about 17 inches long) that lives at depths ranging from 650 to 1,650 feet.*

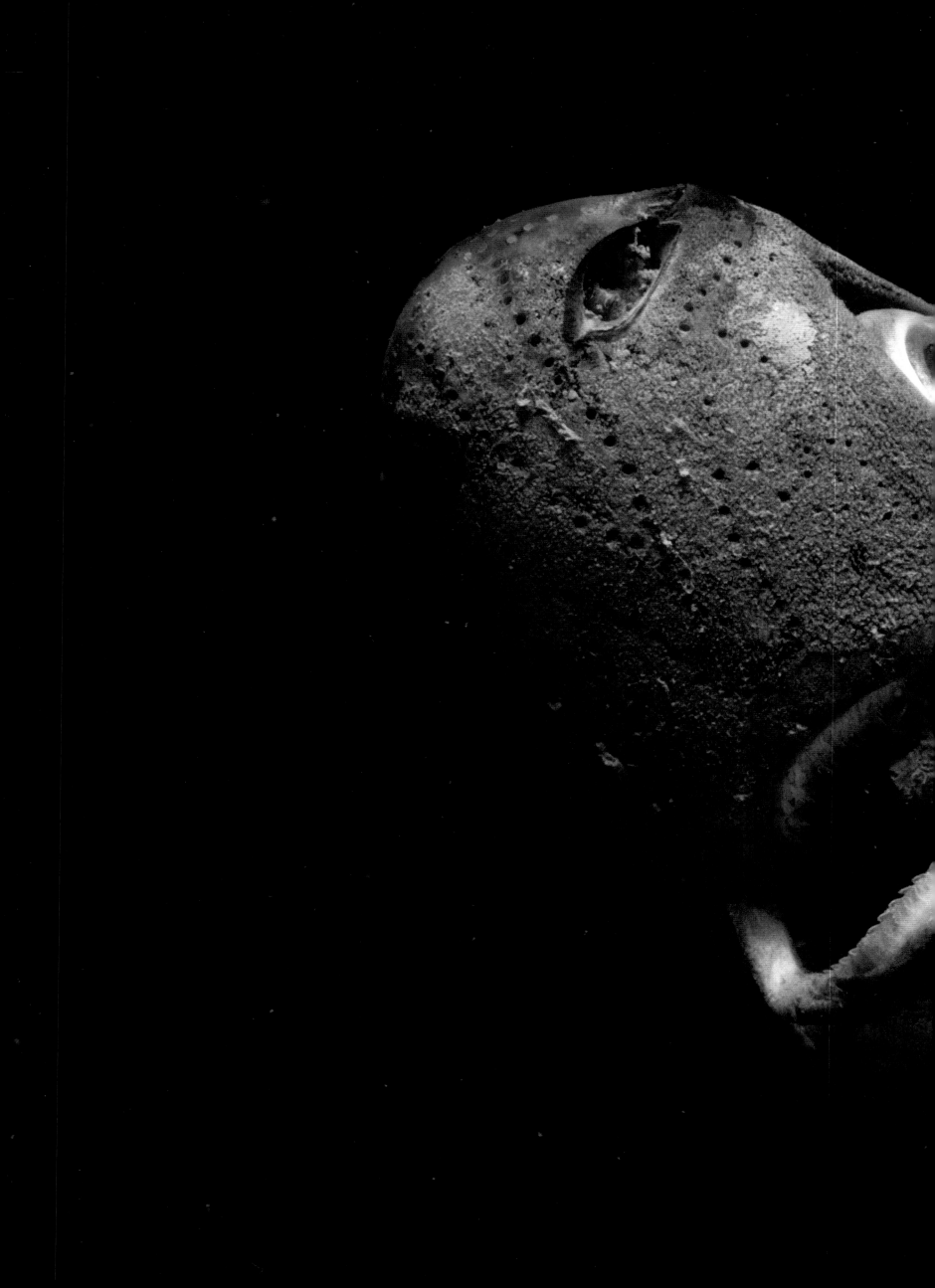

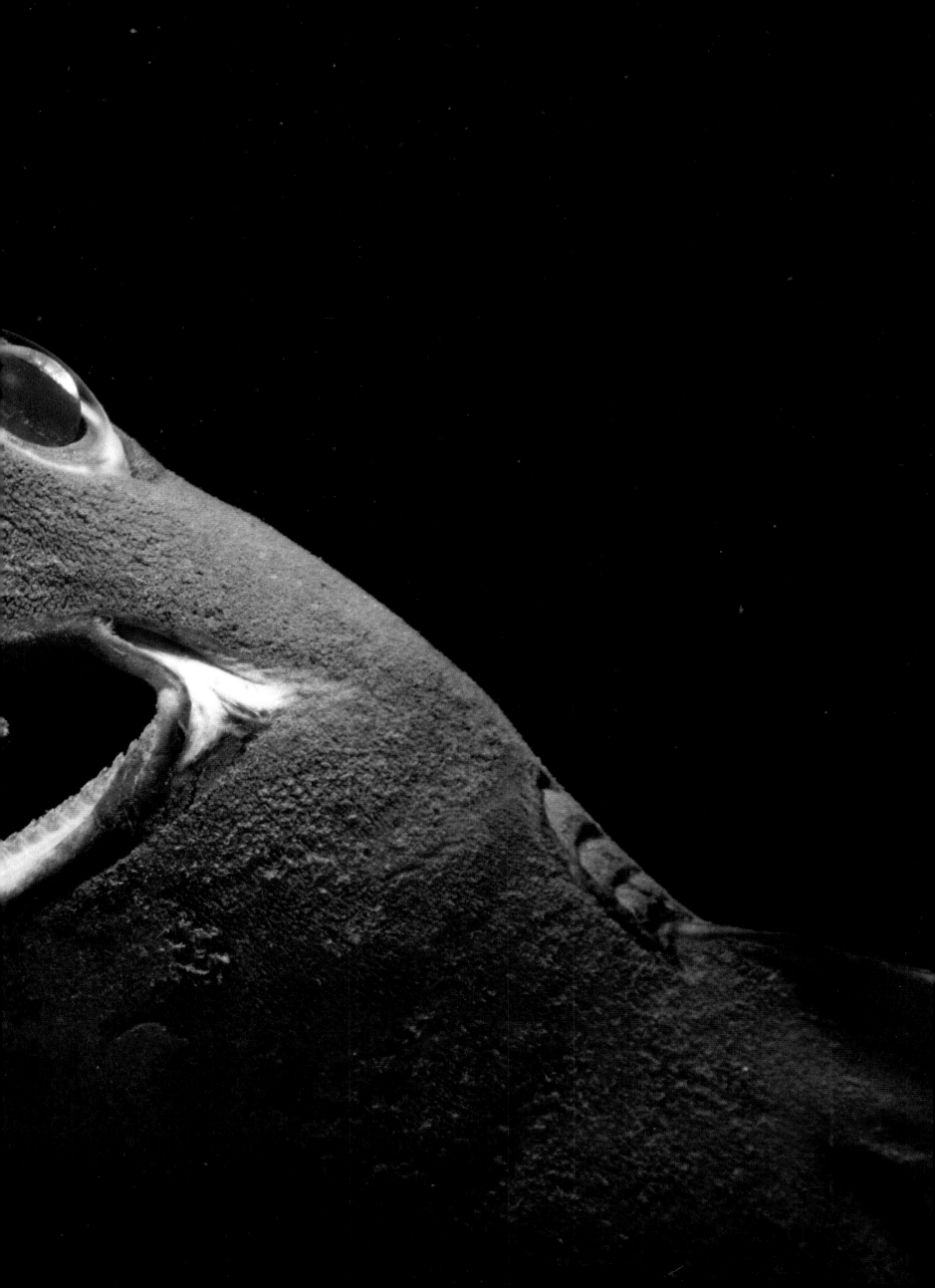

In Harm's Way: Man and the Shark

Gaetano Cafiero

When a black fin sliced through the clear blue water just outside the little marina of Mergellina, in Naples, townspeople and fishermen fled in terror, thinking that the fin was that of a shark. It was nothing more than a dolphin. But when we were children swimming underwater off the Italian coast, we did encounter sharks. The little cat-sharks, resting motionless in the grottoes, were quick to bite when we discovered them and grabbed them vigorously.

Many years later, once we had become full-fledged scuba divers, we went off to test our skill in distant and exotic waters, pulling on the tails of nurse sharks, dragging them out of the grottoes in which they slept. We also managed to pester other, less good-natured sharks as well. Once, in the Maldives, when we needed to complete the shooting of a documentary by Gian Franco Bernabei, we did everything we could to attract some fierce-looking sharks, without the slightest success. Arturo Santoro was harpooning reef fish, especially small jacks, using a harpoon without flanges so that the fish would be shot through—mortally wounded, but not hindered by the harpoon. The fish's desperate frenzy and the blood it lost should have attracted sharks in droves, but Santoro saw only one approaching from the dark blue depths. He directed me straight ahead. I framed the shark in the viewfinder of my camera and waited for it to come within range, but it suddenly stopped about twelve feet away, turned, and disappeared.

And I frankly have no idea of what kind of sharks the fourteen were that surrounded me on the coral shelf of an island in the archipelago of Palau one day in August of 1980. Gian Carlo Giannini, a Florentine and a great underwater hunter, had harpooned a splendid jack among the madrepores of a sea bed some fifty feet beneath the surface of the water, at the edge of an abyss, where the shelf dropped away to a depth of thousands of feet. I had my camera, and both of us were diving without tanks. In the time that it took the harpoon to travel from the gun to the fish, the sharks were upon us in a wheeling black sabbath, none of them longer than six feet, but all of them fast and ruthless in shredding the jack. I distinctly

remember thinking that if just one of those creatures frantically devouring the fish a few meters away were to decide that my leg or my arm looked tasty, there would be absolutely nothing I could do. I understood the complete helplessness of someone who is underwater and faced with sharks in a feeding frenzy: I felt stupid, helpless, frustrated, and terrified.

I also remember the great sense of anxiety shared by those of us on board a deep-sea fishing boat just off Dakar, in Senegal, when a group of great grey fins suddenly appeared and began slicing through the water in ever-smaller circles around our boat, no doubt eyeing the sailfish we had hooked and carefully reeled in close to the hull. And, during that same period, in the village of Saint-Louis, also in Senegal, I went out with a young French engineer who had promised his wife a pink snapper for dinner. We dragged along a diver's balloon with an extra harpoon gun attached to it. I shot a grouper to test the harpoon rifle I had borrowed. When the French diver surfaced with the pink snapper, he asked me to hand him the spare harpoon gun. I pulled the balloon toward me. The cord had been cut clean as if with a sharp knife; both the grouper and the harpoon gun were gone. We floated on the surface for a while with our knees drawn up to our chests, waiting out the sharks, and then we went to fish in safety from a fishing boat crowded with tourists. A man who ran a diving center on Gorée told us that this was normal in Senegal—that scuba divers must always expect to give up a percentage of their catch to the sharks, although there had never been a shark attack on a human as far as he knew. For us, it was sufficient precaution to keep wounded fish hanging from the balloon at a considerable distance and to offer no resistance when the sharks swam in for the prey that had just been taken. We simply had to hand it over, shrug, and let the shark have his meal.

To many people and across many cultures, the shark is regarded as a useless creature of the sea. Those who do not know that most sharks are harmless and that sharks provide many valuable products we use in our daily lives view the shark as purely evil, a killer of men that swallows them

whole. In the stories they perpetuate, the shark reduces humans to naked and helpless creatures; sharks are elevated to mythic proportions, inviting images of vengeful sea devils . . . and even the wrath of God.

Before the ancient Greeks named constellations after figures in their myths, the human imagination had already projected into the stars a number of different depictions of devil-gods—including sharks. The very same collection of stars that the Greeks identified as Orion, the Hunter, were interpreted by the Warran Indians of South America as the missing leg of Nohi-Abassi, a man who had rid himself of his mother-in-law by teaching a shark to attack her and devour her. According to the legend, one of Nohi-Abassi's sisters-in-law, however, then transformed herself into a shark and severed his leg with a single bite. He bled to death, and his leg was left to drift through one part of the heavens while his body drifted through another.

In the Solomon Islands, sharks, which have become deified, live in underwater grottoes carved out especially for them in coastal waters. Vietnamese fishermen still pray to the whale shark as "Lord Fish." And when Pearl Harbor was built, divers discovered a sort of underwater amphitheater, partially submerged, in which the ancient Hawaiian kings, it is said, would order a gladiator, armed with a short dagger made of a shark's tooth set in a wooden handle, to combat a shark. In Japanese mythology, Same-Hito, the shark-man, is the god of storms. In fact, the shark of Japanese legends is so terrifying that the Chinese, when resisting the Japanese invasion of 1937, chose the head of the tiger shark as a talisman to adorn the noses of their fighter planes. American fighter planes in the Pacific had their noses painted as a gaping, tooth-filled shark's mouth.

In Oceania, the shark is regarded as the god of the sea. It is feared but also beloved as a protector ready to assist those humans who put their faith in him. The eighty-five strips of island in the Tuamotu atoll are inhabited by people who lived exclusively from fishing until just a few years ago. And they had to struggle to keep every fish they took from the sea out of the hungry jaws of

RIGHT *It is fairly common for whale sharks, harmless giants of the sea, to allow scuba divers to approach them. Some whale sharks measure as much as fifty feet in length, and reports have been made of individual specimens that attained lengths of up to sixty feet and weighed some twenty tons. These sharks have nothing in common with whales except for their enormous size and the fact that they are filter-feeders. Whale sharks are typically found in warm seas, and only rarely do they venture out of the tropics. Ningaloo Reef, along the western coast of Australia, is one of the areas in which these sharks can most easily be found.*

23, TOP The whale shark is one of the fish least studied by science, perhaps because it has never been hunted extensively and has never been the object of commercial interests. The actual biomass of the whale shark is unknown. As a result, it is difficult to say whether this species is in any way endangered.

sharks. Every strip of bait prepared to trap tuna and jacks is an inviting morsel for these giant, insatiable predators. Yet the relationship between men and sharks in these islands, as close and constant as it is, has always been and continues to be based on fear and veneration—a combination of hatred and devotion. The oral tradition of these islanders is rich with reassuring tales of friendly sharks—sharks that escort an outrigger through the rough waves, sharks that rise rapidly from the gloomy depths to help a human in danger, and more.

Today, sharks are hunted and exploited all over the world and yield vast profits. In 1990 alone, some 709,000 metric tons of sharks were taken from the oceans of the world and exchanged for cold, hard cash. The Chinese use shark fins as the fundamental ingredient in an exotic soup. In Central and Latin America, India, Indonesia, and Malaysia, shark is part of the daily diet. Italy imports tons of blue shark, mako, and blackfin, falsely labeled as swordfish. The tiny piked dogfish, which is caught in massive quantities in the North Atlantic, is the base for the German seafood specialty Schillerlocken, while in England, this same shark is smoked and served in pubs and small restaurants as the "fish" in fish-and-chips.

Sharks are sources of a wide variety of nonedible products as well. Shark liver, which is particularly rich in vitamin A, is a source of squalene, a substance used in the manufacture of cosmetics; it allegedly has miraculous properties that help diminish wrinkles. Sharkskin, called *shagreen*, has a rough, grainy surface similar to sandpaper, and has been used to polish wood. When the denticles are removed from sharkskin, the resulting leather has a high tensile strength and is used in the manufacture of shoes, purses, belts, and other accessories. Sharks' teeth are often set in gold or silver and made into unique, expensive jewelry. The cartilaginous skeleton is the source of a substance used in cancer chemotherapy. The corneas of certain sharks have actually been used as successful substitutes for human corneas. In reality, sharks are far less likely to be the hunters of humans as they are to be the hunted.

TOP LEFT *A sand tiger shark is surrounded by a cloud of smaller fishes, clearly undaunted by its presence. Female sand tiger sharks stop eating when they're ready to give birth; perhaps this is a mechanism that prevents them from devouring their young.*

LEFT *During feeding frenzies, sharks enter an excited state that seems to render them completely indifferent to their surroundings, and in some cases, they actually turn on each other. This phenomenon can chiefly be observed when large quantities of food are dropped into the ocean as bait. The most thorough documentation of this activity has come from the observation of grey reef sharks, which have never been known to make direct attacks on humans during a feeding frenzy.*

The Great White "Terror"

Humans are fascinated by sharks—that much is certain. The earliest depiction of an attack by something which was, in all probability, a great white shark was a painting on a Campanian vase dating from 725 B.C., uncovered during a dig at Ischia, a volcanic island in the Tyrrhenian Sea near Naples. Two-and-a-half centuries after the vase was painted, in 492 B.C., Herodotus wrote a description of a sea monster attacking a man. The Greek historian calls the monster *keté*, which, at the time, commonly signified a sea monster; it principally referred to whales (hence cetacean); no other term was used to describe sharks more specifically. A poet, Leonidas of Taranto, described the tragic demise of Tharsys, a sponge diver who was attacked by a *keté* and bitten in two as he was preparing to climb back into his boat. His fellow sailors buried the upper half of the unfortunate Tharsys, while the lower half was devoured by the horrible monster.

From those early accounts up to the present day, stories of shark attacks provide a long crescendo of terrifying descriptions. In 1580, an English chronicler who set sail in Portugal and headed for India wrote of a man who was swept overboard by the wrath of a typhoon and of the effort to rescue him by throwing him a wooden lifesaver tied to the ship by a line. There was no way of averting disaster: the man had just managed to reach the lifesaver when he was ripped in half by a shark before the horrified eyes of his helpless shipmates.

In 1776, a French scientist named Thomas Pennant wrote a description of the great white shark: "It grows to a considerable size. It is said that in the belly of one of these monsters, an entire human body was once found, which is far from improbable, considering their love of human flesh. They are the nightmare of sailors in all warm-water sailing, where they follow ships incessantly to catch anything that might happen to fall into the water. A man that happened to fall overboard would be without a hope. Sharks have been seen to set upon men like hunting dogs upon a boar. Swimmers are often killed by sharks. At times, they lose only an arm or a leg, while in other cases they are cut clean in two by these insatiable animals."

The fixed stare, the powerful and massive body, the huge serrated triangular teeth—these are the most noteworthy characteristics of the great white shark. In effect, a fish weighing 1,500 pounds (the average weight of a great white) moving at 35 miles per hour, determined to attack its chosen victim, is one frightening predator. The reasons why great white sharks attack humans have not been determined. There are those who think that great whites consider swimmers to be as good a form of prey as any other, especially because there is little in the ocean that a great white would not consider edible. Others believe that many of the great white attacks on humans are mistakes—the shark instinctively attacks a victim, but when it realizes that this is not its usual prey, it withdraws.

The ultimate example of the shark as a vicious predator and an evolutionary perfection of the senses and of form, the great white is known to Australians as the white pointer, to Hawaiians as the Mano Ni-Uhi, and to so many others as, simply, the white death. Of the great white, writer Jim Crockett wrote, "A friend of mine claims to have seen

are dumped into the sea, and when the white pointer shows up, members of the group descend beneath the surface in a steel cage. Through the bars of the cage, they take photographs and aim their video cameras for close-up views of the massive sharks. This is pure folly; if a great white were to attack, no one would be able to escape.

Some of the advice put forth in survival manuals distributed by the armed forces in various parts of the world seems entirely superfluous: they suggest, for example, that the shark be smacked soundly on the snout if it charges. Anyone who has ever been in a shark cage and has seen a female measuring close to sixteen feet and weighing over a ton ripping apart mouthfuls of animal flesh each weighing about forty pounds, anyone who has seen a great white bearing down on the cage with its black, expressionless eyes and with powerful, gaping jaws crammed with row after row of saw-bladed teeth, anyone who has seen these things knows that there is no defense against a direct attack.

Unless the shark is hungry or threatened by a foreign presence, however, it will not attack or kill. We humans are the only living things that kill for sport; other animals attack only to obtain food or to defend themselves and their territory. This appears to be true of the shark. But there is something that makes us feel differently about these creatures. Every culture throughout human history has expressed the fear of being eaten alive by sharks. Certainly all the wild beasts, the carnivores that we consider to be "ferocious," could eat us alive. In the face of a charging lion or a pack of wolves, we can always imagine a way of escaping—a tall tree with high branches that we can climb; a door that we can bolt behind us; a rifle we can lift, load, and fire; or a hatchet we can wield—something, anything to defend ourselves. We are learning that the same is true for defending against sharks; there are ways of escaping and of protecting ourselves, depending on the circumstances and the environment in which the attack occurs. Survivors of shark attacks are living proof that divers who keep their wits about them can live to tell about it.

God. Well, I've seen the great white. I guess we're about even."

Sharkwatching expeditions—specifically aimed at the great white—have become very profitable for a few skilled tour-group organizers in New South Wales. The boat sails out into the open Pacific, where those who signed on might spend a week without seeing either land or sharks. Buckets of blood and chum—animal viscera—

A well-known case is that of Australian Rodney Fox, an expert scuba diver who was attacked in 1963 by a great white approximately ten feet long. In a single bite, the shark took a piece of Fox's left flank. Thanks to a fortunate chain of events, the young diver was in an operating room within the hour, and what the surgeons found was this: the stomach, the rib cage, and the left lung had all been laid open. A four-hour operation and 462 stitches later, Rodney Fox had a good chance of surviving, which he did. He has continued to dive, and he has become one of the world's leading authorities in the field of shark behavior. He works extensively on documentaries and research on his would-be assassin.

Perhaps even more spectacular was the case of a Melanesian fisherman named Iona Asai. A shark seized him by the head, but Asai had the presence of mind to strike repeatedly at the shark's eyes with his hands until the shark finally released him unharmed. These important cases are the subject of international study.

RIGHT *Since it is not always an easy thing to find great white sharks, the "shark-watching" boats often have to trawl about for days in search of the right specimens. When they spot one, they encourage it to venture closer by throwing pieces of animal or fish carcass into the water.*

31, TOP *The bite of sharks is particularly effective because, among other things, the upper jaw can slide out at the appropriate moment. This biting technique has been studied by researchers, who have examined films of it frame by frame. It was in this way that they established that the upper jaw is raised up to forty degrees with respect to the longitudinal axis of the body, the lower jaw is dropped, and the upper jaw thrust forward, exposing the shark's teeth and gums. Each of these various phases lasts no longer than two-tenths of a second.*

32-33 *This great white shark, photographed in the waters off Australia, has cuts and abrasions over much of its body. It is possible that these wounds were inflicted by another shark— possibly even during the mating process.*

36-37 *Although the great white shark may seem to be invincible and invulnerable, like many other animals, its survival is endangered by humans. South Africa is the first country to realize that it is necessary to protect this species and has enacted strict laws for the shark's protection.*

The Tiger with the Black Stripes

The tiger shark is more greatly feared than the great white among those who are familiar with both. In fact, the moniker "man-eater" is more appropriately applied to the tiger shark than to the great white—not because the tiger shark is more ferocious, but primarily because it prefers shallow coastal waters where people go swimming and where fishermen drop their hooks and cast their nets.

The name tiger is taken from the distinctive dark bands that run from the top of the shark's back down along its sides—an unmistakable characteristic that is particularly evident in the younger tiger sharks but fades with increasing age, so that the animal's back eventually takes on a uniform greyish or brownish coloring. Chiefly active in coastal waters, the tiger shark can be found in all the temperate and tropical seas on the planet. It is the most common shark along the coasts of South Africa, in the Philippines, in the Indian and Pacific Oceans, and in the waters of the Caribbean region. In Australia, the shark patrols that survey the ocean in airplanes and helicopters spot five tiger sharks for every shark of another species. Tiger sharks seem to prefer murky waters, volcanic islands, and undersea cliffs with sheer drops plunging straight down to sea beds rich in prey. Nonetheless, they are extremely flexible in tolerating a broad range of different habitats and will as readily go hunting in the estuaries of rivers as in small lagoons.

The enormous and terrifying sea crocodiles that once populated the bay of Wijnkoop on the southern coast of Java were literally driven out in the space of a few years by tiger sharks, although the fishermen of the area did not profit from the exchange. It would appear that the tiger shark prefers hunting by night and spends the daytime hours in deep, cool waters, often hiding in large undersea crevices or grottoes. When the tiger swims, it does so with remarkable power, moving slowly, appearing to be relaxed and even distracted, but in reality it is very much alert: as soon as it singles out its prey, it can attack with blinding speed.

As far as its feeding habits are concerned, the tiger need not be in any way overshadowed by the great white: it eats anything and has even won the nickname "hyena of the seas." Just how dangerous a shark is to humans has a great deal to do with the shark's feeding habits. The tiger shark is on the list of animals considered to be particularly dangerous to humans, because, aside from its physical size and an awesome arsenal of serrated teeth, one may safely say that, in its feeding habits, the tiger is the most opportunistic and indiscriminate shark of all. If a tiger is hungry, it eats whatever crosses its path. This is certainly the least specialized of sharks in terms of diet, and that may in part be because its teeth are so incredibly efficient; some naturalists feel that the tiger has the most effective teeth of any animals considered dangerous to humans. This shark is aided in detecting possible prey by the remarkable expanse of its nostrils, which are quite broad and deep and which bring even the most diluted of aromas to the brain. The tortoise fishermen of the Seychelles Islands tell of having traveled over miles and miles of ocean without seeing a single shark, but no sooner had they dragged several tortoises along in the water than they suddenly found a tiger shark following in the wake of their vessel.

The tiger shark eats a great variety of bony fish, including the tarpon, moray eel, cod, and flounder. It also eats other, smaller sharks, such as the saw shark, the grey reef shark, the hammerhead, and even other tiger sharks, along with most underwater reptiles, especially tortoises, but also sea snakes of the Indian and Pacific Oceans (the extremely powerful venom has no effect on the shark). In the Galápagos Islands, iguanas and seabirds fall prey to tiger sharks. Also at risk are frigate birds, cormorants, pelicans, and other species of migratory birds that come to rest on the ocean surface when the tiger shark is swimming nearby. Among the marine mammals most often attacked by tiger sharks are sea lions, seals, dolphins, and dead or dying whales. Crustaceans and invertebrates known to have been eaten by tiger sharks include crabs, lobsters, and octopuses.

The tiger shark has become especially adept at attacking fish that have been caught by

Among the sharks most feared by humans, the tiger shark is usually second after the great white shark. The name refers to the striped pattern on the tiger shark's dorsal area, which appears as elongated spots in the immature sharks. This is one of the most voracious species known to science; in the stomachs of captured tiger sharks, in fact, an amazing variety of objects have been found. Among the natural prey of tiger sharks are fish, other sharks, rays, sea turtles, dolphins, seals, sea birds, crustaceans, and mollusks. This shark, too, is endangered by humans, who hunt it for its meat, which is considered to be quite a delicacy in the West Indies, and for its skin, which commands high prices for its special quality.

fishermen, either on lines or in nets, and therefore constitutes a major problem for the fishing industry in certain regions. This habit, however, often costs the tiger shark its life, because it not only swallows its prey, but also the hook on which it was caught, and the shark often ends up thrashing on the deck of a fishing boat. This is regarded as fair compensation by the crew of the boat, hurt financially by the tiger's frequent raids: they may give up part of their catch, but the tiger brings something else. The skin of the tiger is the most sought-after of all shark skins, which makes it the most expensive. It yields a leather that is more elastic and stronger than that of cows or pigs. The teeth of tiger sharks also have considerable value in the souvenir trade, where, combined with silver or gold, they are made into jewelry or other ornamentation.

Because of its commercial potential, the tiger shark is hunted by the Indonesians. Using more primitive methods, the inhabitants of the Gilbert Islands hunt the tiger too. They take a short line with a baited hook and directly attach it to a small canoe paddled by a single fisherman. Once the tiger is hooked, the fisherman allows it to wear itself out, so that hours and miles later, the exhausted shark can be dragged on board and killed.

Very little is known about the biology of the tiger shark, a species that, like many others, is difficult to study in its natural environment. From observations made chiefly in the Caribbean, where the tiger is one of the most common types of shark, it has been possible to establish that this shark is nocturnal and that it often ventures into very shallow waters. The tiger shark, which attains a maximum length of eighteen feet, is the largest of all the requiem sharks. Usually distinguished by its slow and majestic pace, it is also capable of sudden starts and lunges and can accelerate very quickly when pursuing prey. Its tail is its chief means of propulsion; the upper lobe is much longer than the lower lobe.

42-43 Even in the absence of the tiger stripes, which tend to fade with age, Gale-ocerdo cuvier can be recognized by its large head, its short snout, and its broad mouth. The teeth are also quite distinctive—serrated at the edges and curved to one side.

The Ragged "Grin" of the Sand Tiger Shark

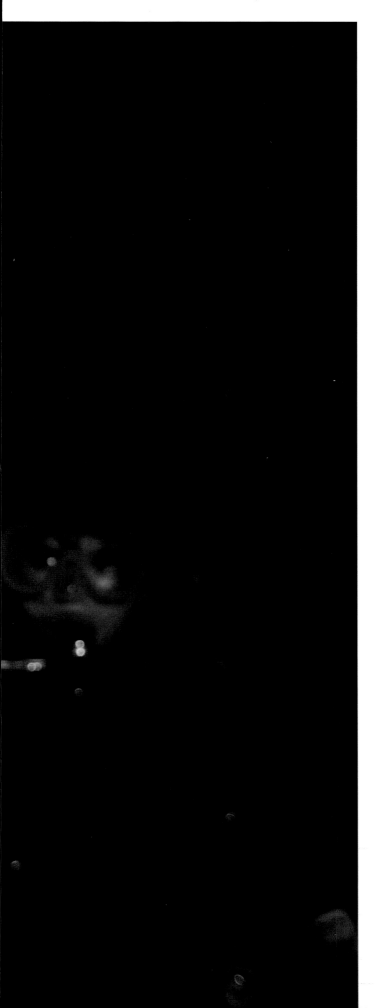

Known to Australians as the grey nurse and to South Africans as the spotted raggedtooth, the sand tiger shark is a frightening spectacle with its mouthful of jagged teeth. The shapes of the teeth vary according to function: the serrated, triangular teeth cut and rip the flesh of prey. In many species, the teeth curve inward and lie almost flat when the shark's mouth is closed. These several rows of irregular teeth are the sand tiger's gruesome "calling card"—this shark has a habit of swimming with its mouth open. Another frightening aspect of this shark's appearance is its yellow eyes with their flat, black pupils.

Found primarily in the shallow waters off the coast, the sand tiger shark is nonetheless a migratory creature that cruises through all of the world's seas, both tropical and temperate, shifting from the Southern to the Northern Hemisphere and back again as the seasons change. During its long migrations, in which it moves along slowly at a variety of depths, the shark rises to the surface and takes great gulps of air and then positions itself at different depth levels by emitting bubbles.

In South Africa, a number of attacks on bathers have been attributed to the sand tiger shark. In Australia, its bad reputation is undeserved. There, the shark is the victim of unprovoked attacks by scuba divers equipped with harpoon rifles—so much so that the species is to some extent endangered.

The sand tiger shark has a particularly frightening appearance because of the numerous rows of teeth protruding from its mouth. In reality, it is not considered to be particularly dangerous to humans. The teeth are rather fine and small and are used in capturing and devouring small prey— chiefly fish, cephalopods, and crustaceans. Tranquil by nature, this shark is found in the Atlantic and off the U.S. coast from Maine to the Gulf of Mexico, as well as from southern Brazil to Argentina, in the Mediterranean, along the west African coast as far south as Cameroon, in the Red Sea, from Japan to Indonesia, and along the coasts of Australia and South Africa.

The sand tiger shark is much sought after by fishermen, especially hook-and-line fishermen; its flesh is used in dishes considered to be delicacies in Japan. This shark is active at night, and during the day it is content to remain on the sea bed. By nature it is not particularly aggressive, and it adapts quite well to captivity, which makes it an ideal subject for scientific observation.

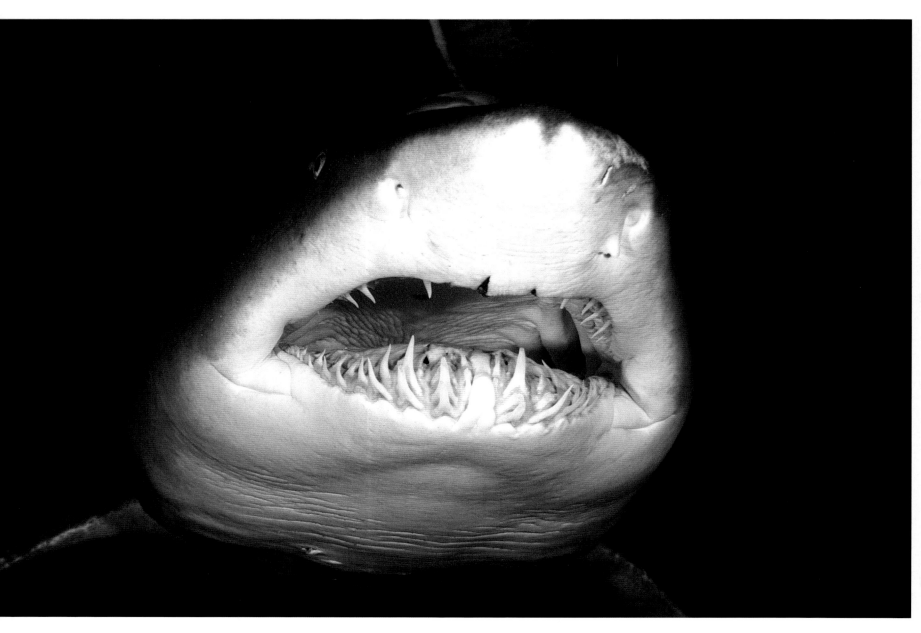

48-49 The size of an adult sand tiger shark is considerable—6.5 to 9.5 feet in length. The longest sand tiger shark ever measured was just over 10 feet from snout to tail. The young of the species are about three feet long at birth.

The Mysterious Hammerhead

In the Sea of Cortez, in Mexico, on the famous shallows of El Bajo, hammerhead sharks assemble in huge groups at certain times of the year. More than 200 sharks of the species Sphyrna lewini *gather for reasons that are yet to be determined. Researchers hypothesize that the phenomenon may be linked either to migration or reproduction. Large schools of hammerhead sharks can be*

The sea becomes cloudy as if before a storm. Viewed from the depths below, the light from the surface fades as dozens of hammerheads come swirling onto the scene in a sudden, startling moment. They swim together as if they are being urgently summoned to a mysterious destination. It is a breathtaking sight to see. But as quickly as they arrive, the hammerheads are gone; they vanish into the depths, the light filters through from the surface once again, and the sea regains its brilliant blue color. Large gatherings of hammerheads are not unusual, although the reasons for this behavior are not fully understood.

depths ranging from sixteen to one hundred feet, hundreds of hammerheads from six to thirteen feet in length swim by in a northerly direction at an unchanging velocity of several knots. The timing appears to be affected by the direction of the winds, the water temperature, and other factors.

Several theories have been put forth regarding the reasons for these large gatherings. Hammerheads apparently single out clearly defined areas within their hunting territories, where they remain for the entire period in which they are not feeding. The behavior could be linked to the hunt for specific types of food, or it could also be related to the reproduction cycle in some way. And it should be pointed out that although hammerheads are the most frequently sighted undersea migrators in these waters, other marine creatures do make the same trip in the same direction; these include rays, manta rays, larger species of bony fish, and even whales. The sharks making this journey have never shown the slightest sign of hostility to humans who dive to watch them go by. Although hammerheads are very sensitive to sudden noises, the sounds of underwater cameras do not appear to disturb them.

Some researchers have hypothesized that hammerheads may gather in other specific geographic areas but at great depths, where humans cannot observe them. Relationships between individual members of shark groups have been observed in which dominant and submissive roles have been demonstrated. In this context, it has been hypothesized that the periodic assemblies of hammerheads in the Sea of Cortez could serve, on the one hand, to protect the smaller hammerheads from the aggression of the larger ones, and on the other, to establish hierarchic roles that serve to ensure the continuation of the species.

observed in other regions as well, such as the Galápagos Islands. Depending on the species, sharks belonging to the genus Sphyrna *range in length from just over three feet to eighteen feet. The species pictured here is perhaps the most common of all the hammerheads; it lives in tropical seas and stays close to coastlines and islands.*

The first person to capture a gathering of hammerheads on film was Ramon Bravo, a talented Mexican underwater filmmaker. The sequence was seen all over the world in a film directed by Bruno Vailati. The film was made in an attempt to debunk some of the myths surrounding these and other ocean creatures that have been labeled as evil or dangerous, often through mere ignorance.

These fantastic processions are known to follow very predictable schedules. The Mexican divers who work as guides in the Sea of Cortez know the exact date and time a grouping will occur. Just a short distance from the shore, at

In the chapter on hammerheads, published in the fourth volume, parts one and two, of the *Fisheries Synopsis No. 125—Sharks of the World*, published by the FAO, the United Nation's Organization on Food and Agriculture, placed alongside the silhouette and the scientific data on the hammerhead there is a symbol that indicates that these sharks pose at least a minimal threat to humans. Hammerheads are

found in every warm temperate and tropical sea throughout the world. A maximum of thirteen feet in length, they live on bony fish, cephalopods, and rays. That they are considered to be dangerous, or at least potentially dangerous, may be the result of their being confused with their close relatives, the great hammerheads.

The great hammerhead—rare but not entirely absent in temperate waters—may grow longer than nineteen feet. That alone is enough to win it not one but two symbols from the FAO. Otherwise, this shark's behavior is similar to that of its smaller cousin. In terms of prey, it shows a clear preference for the stingray, apparently unaffected by the ray's powerful defense mechanism— a sharp spine on the back of its whiplike tail through which it delivers a potent poison. One hammerhead that found its way into the nets of a trawler had fifty of these spines penetrating its tongue, throat, and palate.

In many islands of the Indian and Pacific oceans, sharks have been sanctified for generations. In New Zealand, the Maori have chosen to place the hammerhead among their gods. In the Maori tongue, the hammerhead is called *Mangopare* and is considered to bring good luck. In the Pacific islands, a great many fantastic shark tales have been handed down, and one of them would have it that sharks are reincarnations of dead humans: perhaps the immense schools of sharks that swim slowly and solemnly through the underwater world are simply clouds of souls, as in some underwater paradise in which the spirits manifest themselves in disquieting shapes.

It is not known why hammerheads, so similar in some ways to other sharks, should have evolved their strange, T-shaped heads. The fact that their eyes and nares, or nasal openings, lie at each end of the "hammer" suggests that these sharks have extreme stereoscopic vision and a stereoscopic sense of smell. Another explanation could be that the spread-out head serves to increase the surface area over which the electroreceptors are distributed; these serve to detect prey hidden under the sand. Other possible advantages of having a head shaped like a hammer may be an increase in maneuverability, or the increased buoyancy provided by the "wing effect." It also may simply be a deterrent designed to frighten off aggressors. In all likelihood, though, the functions of this bizarre structure are probably more than one. The shape of the head may actually pose a disadvantage: it is a fairly delicate structure that can be easily damaged by other sharks.

54-55 Sphyrna mokarran is the largest species of all hammerhead sharks and can grow to nearly twenty feet. The shape of the head is very rectangular.

BELOW *Within the category of sharks, the family of the hammerheads is considered by paleontologists to be the most recent in evolutionary terms. Reconstruction of fossils is particularly difficult* *in the case of cartilaginous fish—all that remains of them, for the most part, is their teeth. But it is believed that the Sphynidae first appeared only about 25 million years ago.*

RIGHT *A hammerhead shark swims along accompanied by a school of Creole fish.*

57, TOP Although they tend to prefer deeper waters, hammerhead sharks at times venture into the shallows along the coastline. The young of the species are often sighted near the shore in tropical and warm, temperate areas.

58-59 This picture documents a thrilling faceoff between a scuba diver and a hammerhead shark. The larger species are considered to be potentially dangerous; the Shark Attack File lists a number of cases of unprovoked attacks against people and boats.

The Magnificent Mako

The mako shark is a close "relative" of the great white but is not considered to be as dangerous. Like the great white, the mako is capable of keeping its body temperature higher than the surrounding environment. This gives the shark a particular degree of efficiency, and as

a result, it can swim at very high speeds. The mako shark is very common in tropical and temperate seas, both along the coasts and in open waters.

The fishermen of the Gilbert Islands, as proof of their virility, will sometimes challenge a tiger shark in a duel. They approach their foe armed with tricks learned through experience and lore—and with a dagger clenched in their teeth. But these daring fishermen would never challenge a mako shark with the same confidence. A deep, dark blue on the back and snowy white on the belly, sleek, well-proportioned, fast, fearless, and aggressive, the mako of the Indian and the Pacific oceans is one of the handsomest creatures in the water. This species is practically identical to the one found in the Atlantic Ocean and the Mediterranean Sea. Both species inhabit the area ranging from New Zealand to central California, in the Pacific Ocean, and from Argentina to Nova Scotia in the Atlantic.

Like a great many other sharks, the mako can be found in much higher latitudes in late summer, but it is in the warm tropical and subtropical waters that the mako demonstrates its deadly aggressiveness. The mako is the largest fish sought out by sports fishermen in North America, who claim that the mako is the only shark that will ignore a rotting carcass hanging over the side of a stationary boat for a chance to chase and catch a baited hook trailing from a moving sportsfishing boat. Therefore, fishermen lure and catch makos with a basic technique not unlike that used for tuna, marlin, sailfish, and other large fish. The technique involves scattering blood and chopped fish into the water and the preparation of the bait in such a way that, as it is dragged through the water by the boat, it skips along the surface of the water as if it were still alive. The bait is kept at a certain distance from the boat by the use of outriggers. When the shark takes the bait, the fisherman must quickly fasten himself into his seat, firmly yet carefully letting out the line and then slowly reeling it back in, inch by inch, working to tire the shark without breaking the line. The mako fights like a true adversary, leaping frantically out of the water, high into the air, and slapping back onto the waves. Ernest Hemingway described such a struggle from firsthand experience; he held a world record for catching a 750-pound mako just off Bimini in the Bahamas in 1936.

Whereas the tiger shark will swim lazily toward its prey, the great white will rush head down toward it, and the blue shark will swim around it suspiciously, the mako will dart toward a fish it believes to be alive, chase it, and then stab at it relentlessly. Not even after a mako has been captured, tossed onto the deck of the boat, and clubbed can one be certain that it has been safely vanquished; the mako is capable of lying motionless and apparently lifeless and then turning and suddenly lashing out to savage whatever hapless individual is within reach of its terrible jaws. Although the mako prefers the open sea, in some cases it ventures close to shore, and it even comes into harbors and marinas, especially when it is hunting sardines, cod, or herring. The intense dark blue on the back of the mako, which seems brighter in the glitter of the sun on the surface of the water, harmonizes perfectly with the environment preferred by this splendid and powerful creature. In the open Atlantic, in the heart of the great Gulf Stream, it is not uncommon to spot the dorsal fin of the mako as it slices through the surface of the water.

A "Litter" of Lemon Sharks

The sickle-fin lemon shark *(Negaprion acutidens)* lives off the coastline of the Indian Ocean, off Madagascar, India, Sri Lanka, Malaysia, Indonesia, and western Australia. The lemon shark *(Negaprion brevirostris)* is a uniquely American shark: it lives off the temperate coasts of the United States, both Atlantic and Pacific, and in one instance has been known to extend as far south as South America. The waters of the Caribbean seem to constitute its chosen haunts, especially for reproduction. Although lemon sharks are requiem sharks, they are not aggressive by nature. Like most of the other Carcharinidae, they are viviparous.

Sharks may be considered primitive in many ways, but when it comes to propagating the species, they display a great determination and adaptability. Whereas bony fish scatter millions of eggs through the water, of which only a fraction survive, sharks produce far fewer "pups," and some sharks bring only one of those to term. The baby shark is already capable of taking care of itself from the moment it is born.

Some species—the bull shark, the great white, and the thresher shark—present a remarkable feature, intrauterine cannibalism, or oophagia. The first embryo to develop begins to devour all the other embryos present in the uterus until it is left alone until it is born, the product of a very sophisticated process of natural selection. Among the ovoviviparous, the eggs are incubated and hatch in the belly of the mother. Each embryo is connected to the yolk sac by means of a yolk stalk.

In this remarkable sequence of photographs, taken in the waters off the Bahamas, a scuba diver assists a lemon shark who is giving birth. One after another, ten young lemon sharks (Negaprion brevirostris) *are "delivered." The adult female, just over six-and-a-half feet in length, was caught by a fisherman's hook-and-line, and the stress of the experience probably triggered these premature births. In the photograph at top right, the young shark is still attached to the umbilical cord. In many species of sharks, the method of reproduction is similar to that of mammals: the young develop inside the mother's body, through which they receive nourishment for the entire period of gestation. Unlike mammals, however, once the little sharks are born, they receive no care from their mothers and have to fend for themselves from the moment they are born. Research performed on lemon sharks has shown that the young tend to remain in a restricted area initially. As they grow, they gradually expand their territory.*

64-65 Lemon sharks are common along both the eastern and western coasts of the United States. They have also been observed along the western coast of Africa.

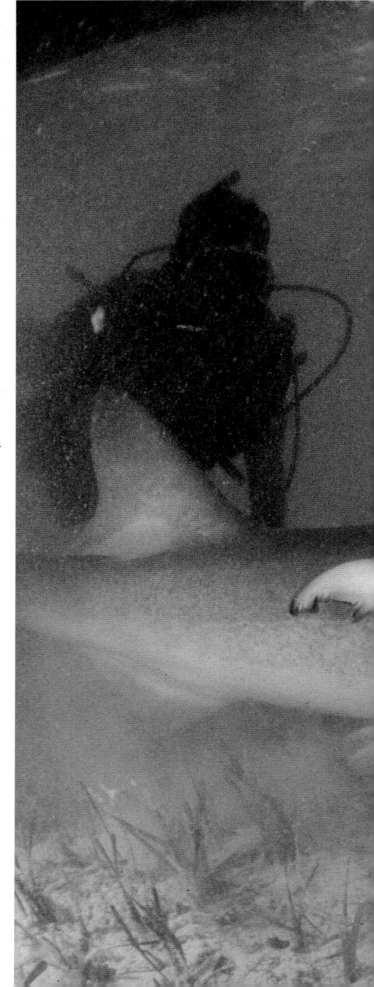

A Flash of Blue
in the Deep

An intense dark blue on its back, a luminous, lighter blue along its flanks, and bright white on its belly, the great blue shark is slim and sleek with long, tapered pectoral fins. It is the most widely traveled of all sharks; with a tremendous range, it swims through all the oceans and seas in the world. By night, in temperate waters, this shark goes exploring along the coasts in large groups, especially when those coasts are frequented by schools of fish and cephalopods, specifically sardines and squid—the basic elements of the blue shark's diet. The blue shark prefers cool water; outside of the tropics (north of the Tropic of Cancer and south of the Tropic of Capricorn), in order to find these temperatures, the great blue must live at depths ranging from 250 to 700 feet.

The greatest length this shark attains is slightly less than thirteen feet, although there are reports of individuals over fifteen feet and even up to twenty feet. The great blue shark attains sexual maturity at five years and often lives to be twenty. It is viviparous (it bears live young) and can accommodate anywhere from 4 to 135 embryos in its uterus. In order to conceive, the female must endure a violent coupling, with savage bites delivered by the frantic male. For this reason, the female's skin is three times thicker than that of her male partner. In the Pacific Ocean, this shark often assembles in crowds and packs, especially between 20 degrees and 50 degrees north latitude. The blue shark migrates across the Atlantic in numerous large schools, either toward Europe following the Gulf Stream, or toward the Caribbean, with the help of the north-equatorial current.

In 1967, eleven years after the Andrea Doria sank off the New York coast, Italian diver Bruno Vailati organized the first underwater inspection of the wreck. In preparation for the dive, he gave a great deal of thought to the blue sharks. Stefano Carletti, who was twenty-seven at the time, was chosen to be the "anti-shark bodyguard" to Vailati, while he shot his footage, and to American diver Al Giddings as he shot his underwater still photographs. Carletti's job was to allow them to work without worrying about the nosy—and dangerous—inhabitants of the undersea relic. The following year, Carletti published a book about the experience, in which he wrote the following: "we personally saw only blue sharks, but we always considered it possible that the other great and dangerous predators, great white sharks, might show up. In fact, we were not far from Montauk, the kingdom of this species, and moreover, we had heard of attacks occurring even at temperatures as low as the ones at which we were working. . . . My job was to protect my fellow divers from sharks. For this purpose, I had an aluminum staff, a by-product of the airplane industry. The head of the staff was made of the finest maritime brass, shaped like a pyramid, and was without flanges. It featured three particularly brutal slicing blades. This tool is usually called a shark billy, and it is extremely effective." So, while Carletti was not particularly concerned about the blue sharks, he was very alert to the possibility of great white sharks, which they were certainly quite likely to encounter in the Atlantic at that depth of 240 feet and which might well be guarding the hull of the sunken ship. In the end, the divers who took part in that expedition were not attacked, although there were great blues swarming all over the wreck.

Nor did the blue sharks particularly impress these divers, who take part every summer in the Italian sharkfishing championship. The blue shark is the only prey of this competition, which is organized by a builder of pleasure craft and one who is especially interested in attracting those who participate in deep-sea fishing. For some years now, the competition has taken place under the auspices of Big Game Italia, a sportsmen's association that practices tag-and-release, in which the fisherman fastens a small pink identification tag onto the dorsal fin of the fish caught by hook-and-line fishing and then tosses the fish back into the sea. All of the sharks captured are, in fact, carefully brought on board, tagged by a biologist, and released into the sea. When they are caught once again in another location, they will supply research scientists with useful information about shark migration and distribution.

The reason for the popularity of the great blue is that, when hooked, it leaps high out of the ocean, soaring momentarily above the waves.

Remoras often attach themselves to sharks and other large vertebrates by means of a special suction cup that is actually a modified dorsal fin. It was once believed that these "sharksuckers" were "hitchhiking" in the hopes of eating "leftovers"; in reality many remoras simply dine on the parasites present on their hosts.

FACING With its large, round eyes, long, pointed snout, and pectoral fins that resemble the wings of an airplane, the great blue shark (Prionace glauca) is perhaps one of the easiest sharks to recognize. The name comes from the bluish cast to its back. The great blue is probably the most common cartilaginous fish in the world; it can be found in all seas except the polar seas.

ABOVE *In the waters off California, great blue sharks have been closely studied to determine their habits, behavior, and methods of attack.*

FACING *Australian divers Ron and Valerie Taylor have developed a remarkable anti-shark wet suit that is not unlike the chain mail worn by medieval warriors; it consists of a "coat of armor" made up of thousands of small, stainless steel links that are joined together to make a dense mesh.*

70-71 Great blue sharks are studied through marking, release, and recapture. Individual sharks caught by hook-and-line sports fishermen are marked with an identifying tag and then released. In this way, it has been possible to establish that these sharks tend to move in a clockwise direction through the Atlantic, assisted by the currents.

Moreover, given its habit of studying its prey warily rather than seizing it impulsively, it treats the sports fisherman's bait the same way, sniffing it and approaching it gradually, drawing ever-diminishing circles around it, keeping the fisherman on the edge of his seat, and generally making the "game" more interesting.

Unlike a number of other sharks, the blue shark does not have a particularly terrifying set of teeth. Although it is not a big shark in terms of its bulk (because of its tapered shape, it weighs less at a given length than other sharks of different species), it is sufficiently "great" to be perceived as a worrisome visitor. And this shark is not preceded by the most reassuring of reputations: blue sharks are alleged to have attacked swimmers and fishing boats, although experts do not agree on its harmful nature. In Hawaii, the blue shark is called Mano Inuwaa, which means "nose and canoe," a name that stems from the shark's remarkable habit of intercepting dugouts in the open sea and laying its snout across the outrigger as if to rest. In Tahiti, they consider the blue shark to be the shade, or spirit, of the Handsome Shark, the fiancé of the goddess Taarea, who floats in the sky, eating clouds and dark areas of the Milky Way.

The Italian National Scuba Expedition to the Red Sea took place between 1952 and 1953, during which filmmaker and naturalist Folco Quilici made his first film, *The Sixth Continent.* During this period, the blue shark showed the most alarming behavior of all the sharks encountered. Those were early days—the dawn of underwater exploration. Bruno Vailati, Quilici himself, and others who are now legendary, such as Raimondo Bucher, were all seeing their first sharks, and they were freely attacking nurse sharks and manta rays, shooting them with harpoons launched from primitive spring guns. Just twenty years later, those same divers were renouncing their own actions and the wholesale slaughter, admitting that they had behaved the way they had out of ignorance. Now they are all crusaders for the protection of sharks, for the rights of sharks, which are no different from any other living creature, to be free from attack and from senseless slaughter.

Experiment on the Reef

The same men who, forty years ago, slaughtered sharks for sport, challenging them on their own turf with an underwater rifle in hand—and the young men who learned from those early divers—today photograph sharks. They hand-feed them, holding out to the shark's darting jaws tiny pieces of fish held between two fingers or even clenched in the diver's teeth. All of these men have a healthy respect for sharks; they fear them, but they now know them infinitely better than they did a few decades back. And these men have even learned to love sharks and to list them, regretfully, among the many victims of man's ecological folly. One of these men is Marco Eletti. He wanted to become a friend to sharks.

The sharks would wait for him to leave and then they would dine undisturbed on the fish he had brought. Eletti began to notice that a specific pattern was developing; the sharks seemed to have a sort of internal clock: they would approach him after no fewer than thirty minutes, when the air in his single ten-liter tank was beginning to run short. After the first half-hour, the sharks would gather around him in a circle, as if to tell him that it was time to drop the sack of fish and leave.

Eletti acquired a larger air tank and went down to see what would happen. When the usual half-hour was up, the sharks gathered around him in an unbroken circle. They wanted what was in the bag, although they were not yet ready to close in on the provider. In a few days' time, they had become accustomed to the new schedule, and they changed their pattern. They learned that in order to get the fish, they would have to wait forty-five minutes instead of thirty. It was a step forward. A relationship had been established—a kind of communication between Eletti and the sharks. This diver had in fact managed to learn the language of the deep: he had succeeded in deriving valuable information from the details of this ritual.

On subsequent dives, he turned his attention to other underwater creatures as well. He noted the rhythm of the coral fish as they swam by, the bold "stares" of the barracuda, and the passive indifference of the tuna. He watched the manta rays glide tranquilly by and the moray eels slither lazily along the reef. He claimed this partic-

ular spot as his laboratory. It was the most spectacular reef he had ever seen; it was astonishingly rich in undersea life—coral, fish of many species, eels, and crustaceans. And of course there were the sharks. The area was filled with grey reef sharks. Marco had named it "Shark Thila." This was where he had begun his experiments, his efforts at communication with grey sharks, carried on with a bagful of dead fish.

He soon discovered that the school of sharks that lived there, at a depth of about 130 feet, consisted of some thirty individuals, all female. This piece of information proved to be valuable later on. The dominant shark in the school would be the strongest, the most aggressive, and the least afraid to approach Eletti. "If I can make her my friend, then I will win the trust of all the others," Eletti decided. And he began to bring the sack of dead fish underwater with him once again.

It was during dive number 2,427 that the sea suddenly seemed to change. It had been a strange dive; everything seemed to be moving in slow motion. All of the fish he usually observed seemed to be lethargic—indifferent to his presence. Then, suddenly, the sea burst into frenetic activity. Everything was in turmoil, and the water was filled with fish in flight, flashing and darting

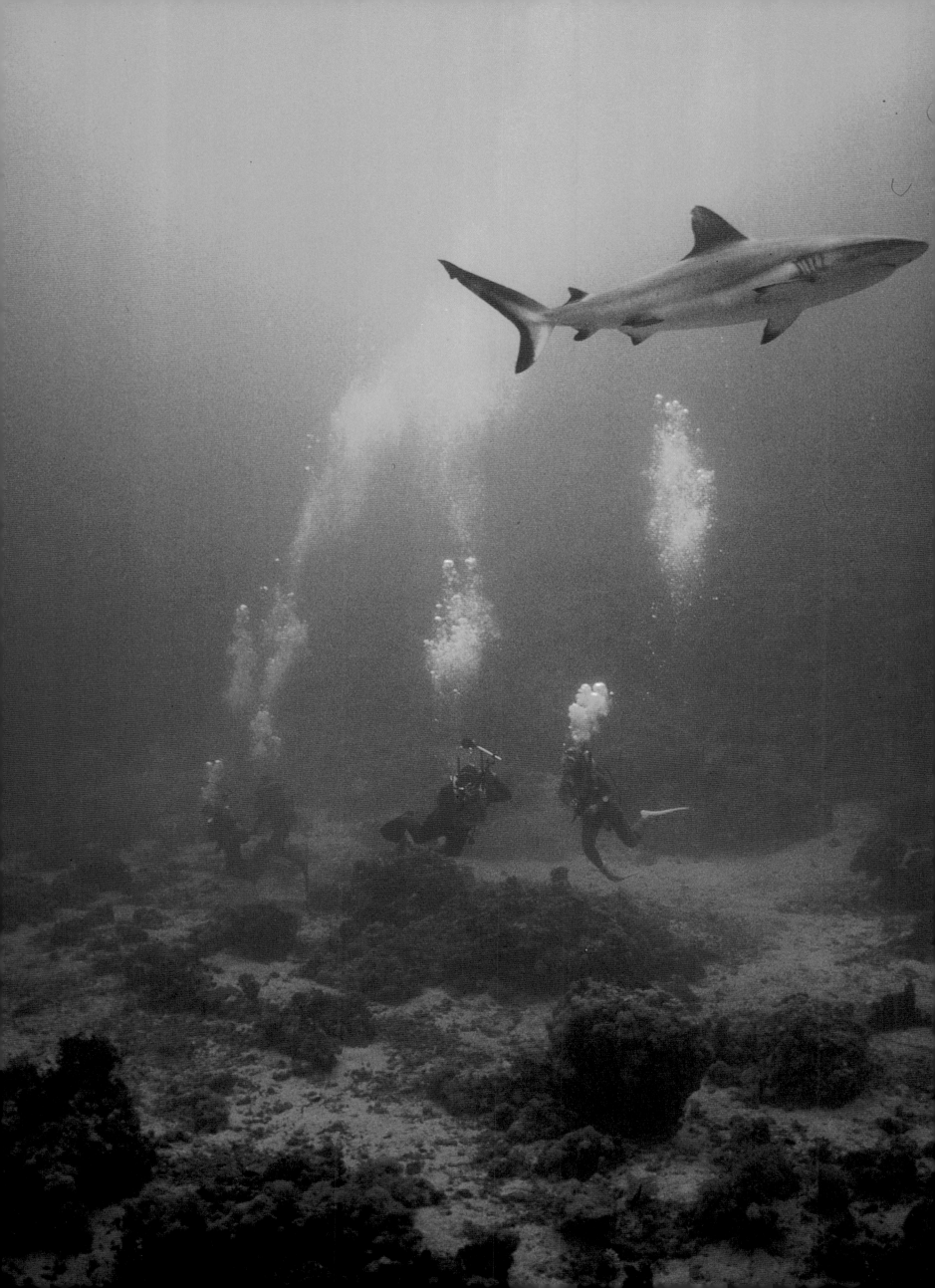

about in a kind of frenzy. And straight out of the deep-blue depths came the school of grey reef sharks. They came forth confidently; it was not their usual elliptical and diffident approach. And they were headed straight for Eletti; their eyes seemed to be fixed on him with a single-minded-ness of purpose. Eletti lifted his hand, holding up a fish filet. What he saw next made him deeply afraid. The dominant shark was approaching very rapidly, and the nicitating membrane that protects a shark's eye while it feeds was closing over hers as she drew nearer. It was clear that the leader was coming in for the fish.

What worried Eletti most was that the sharks would sense his fear. That would constitute a death warrant. He knew that the fastest way to fall prey to a school of sharks was to show fear. It was not the first time he had been in a dangerous situation with sharks. His mind raced, and sud-denly an absurd idea occurred to him just as the lead shark was closing in. He held out the fish and let it fall, and then with the same hand, he grabbed the shark's snout, halting her forward progress, pulled her sharply toward his mouth, and bit her. Eletti alleges that the shark froze, transfixed, as if she had been bitten by a male shark prior to mating.

Grey sharks swim menac-ingly around the sea beds of Rangiroa in the Archipelago of Tuamotu. In all of Poly-nesia, the natives learn as children about dealing with sharks; at times they close off the entrances of the lagoons, imprisoning the sharks, and establish a rela-tionship with them, feeding them every day. At Ran-giroa, the most exciting encounters with sharks occur in the passes of Tipu-ta, Avatoru, and Tivaru, along the northern coasts of the island, where the sharks rise up from the depths in search of food.

76-77 A group of sharks swims just beneath the surface of the water. The family Carcharhinidae includes about forty-eight different species, which vary in length from under three feet to well over thirteen feet. Their distribution is quite wide-ranging; they are present along tropical reefs and in the open sea.

TOP *A grey reef shark swims just beneath the sun-bright surface of the water.*

BOTTOM *Shortnose black-tail reef sharks swim in the Red Sea, off the Sudanese coast.*

RIGHT *On the ocean floor just off the Bahamas, a grey reef shark cautiously observes the diver taking this photograph.*

Cuts and abrasions can be observed on the skin of these white-tip reef sharks (Triaenodon obesus). These were most likely caused by the violent nature of their mating, during which the male bites the female. For this reason, the female has a particularly thick skin, more than twice as thick as that of the male.

84-85 A reef shark glides along just beneath the surface of the water; attached to the left side of the shark's belly is the inevitable remora, barely visible here as a dark outline.

The Nurse Shark: A "Sleeper"

The nurse shark (known by that name in all parts of the world) is a kind of carpetshark. Its back is a brownish grey, and its belly is a dirty white. Other carpetsharks tend to have a far more distinctive coloration, many with spots that help them blend in with their surroundings as they lie motionless on the sea floor. Like other carpetsharks, nurse sharks are bottom-dwellers; they settle onto the bottom in shallow waters, often partially hidden in a grotto from which they tend to dangle their tails. In some cases, groups ranging in size from three to thirty individuals of the same species will pile on top of one another to rest during the day. When night falls, the hunt begins. Nurse sharks prey on small fishes, cephalopods, and crustaceans.

Although it would not appear to be one of the more dangerous sharks, the nurse shark has, from time to time, been known to attack swimmers and divers. Most often, these attacks are in retaliation for some overt act on the part of the "victim." Indeed, many divers find it difficult to resist the temptation to sit astride a nurse shark that seems to be sleeping on the sea floor and even to pose so that a fellow diver can snap a quick picture. Divers have been known to launch a harpoon at the hide of these motionless sharks, only to have the harpoon bounce off the tough hide as if it were a child's toy. When the nurse shark finally rebels against this kind of treatment, the ensuing bite, while it is rarely fatal, is a protracted and terrifying experience: the nurse shark, rather than taking a piece of flesh and swimming away to devour it, sinks its teeth into its victim and tenaciously holds on. The shark has small teeth, adapted for crushing the shells of the small animals on which it feeds, but the muscles of its mouth and jaws are extremely powerful. The nurse shark may appear docile as it rests on the sea floor, but when provoked, it can become a formidable adversary.

This shark is often found near the sea bed, swimming lazily or lying languidly on the sea floor beneath the coral. The nurse shark is generally considered to be harmless, but its tiny teeth can inflict a very painful bite.

88-89 The barbels on the snout and the nasoral grooves are the most distinctive features of the nurse shark. The tail has a distinctive shape as well, with the upper lobe noticeably larger than the lower lobe. Ginglymostoma cirratum, the best-known species of nurse shark, is common in Florida and in the Caribbean Sea.

The Catshark: The "Calico" of the Deep

The catshark is a type of ground shark. Its appearance is somewhat unusual, with its elongated, cat-like eyes and narrow, tapered body covered with colorful and variegated patterns of spots. In areas such as the Tyrrhenian Sea, the catshark is the only shark most people ever see; in these waters, swimmers and divers will rarely, if ever, see the fin of a true "man-eater." Therefore, the role of the shark, in the imaginations of the local people and in the fantasies and nightmares of beginning scuba divers, is played by catsharks.

The name catshark is probably derived from the shark's small, catlike teeth and the mottled coloration of its skin (similar to the "calico" of calico cats). These sharks lie sleeping on the sea floor, often in the shadow of a grotto just a few yards beneath the surface, during the day, and hunt at night. In the resting state, they almost appear inviting, as if to invite a diver to draw near and touch them. But these sleepy-looking sharks can suddenly lash out and deliver a painful bite with their sharp little teeth or an abrasive nudge with their rough skin.

In the past, catsharks have fallen prey in great numbers to novice scuba divers on the prowl. For these divers, who may have been frustrated after failed attempts to capture the trophy they were really after, to have come upon a handsome catshark lying fast asleep on the sea bed, defenseless but for its camouflage, was a temptation too hard to resist. All too often, they harpooned the shark and returned to the surface with their "prize."

Fortunately, this activity did not continue for long. The catshark is not included in underwater hunting competitions, and scuba divers, who have matured in the meantime, have discovered that in the underwater kingdom there were other things to do besides hunting and killing. They've also learned to respect the catshark.

"Catshark" is a popular term for any shark that belongs to the family Scyliorhinidae. The true catshark is the small-spotted catshark, which is found throughout the Mediterranean, in the Eastern Atlantic as far north as Norway and as far south as Senegal, in the North Sea, and in the English Channel. The nursehound shark occupies

the same habitat. The blackmouth catshark, which moves no farther south in the Atlantic ocean than Madeira, appears to prefer murky sea bottoms, at depths of between 600 and 3,000 feet, and is a carnivore that will loosen itself from the soft mud and go hunting, floating along in the middle depths. The others feed exclusively in the bottom pastures, eating small fish, crustaceans, and mollusks.

Most catsharks are oviparous and lay egg capsules that are then anchored to seaweed and other underwater growths by a long stem. The exception is the blackmouth, which simply deposits its eggs in the mud.

This shark often winds up on restaurant menus as "rock salmon" and is actually quite tasty. But the catshark is most sought after for its skin, which is valued for its rough, abrasive surface—excellent for finishing wood and even for polishing stone.

ABOVE *A shark embryo in an early stage of development is still attached to the yolk sac upon which it will feed until birth.*

FACING *This is one of the most amazing sights to be found in the world of sharks—developing catshark embryos. Catsharks are small, fairly harmless sharks whose eggs consist of elongated cases that are transparent when held to the light. The egg cases are often attached to coral or other naturally occurring structures.*

92-93 A young catshark emerges from the casing that has been its home for a number of months.

This unusual shark is a wobbegong. The six or so species belonging to the family Orectolobidae are found chiefly along the coasts of Australia, Papua New Guinea, and Japan.

They tend to be found in the warm waters of the coral reefs. Timid and harmless, they spend much of their time on the sea bed. The Orectolobus ornatus can grow to be almost ten feet long.

The zebra shark (Stegostoma fasciatum) *owes its name to the fact that the skin of its young has a characteristic striped coloration. The adult, in contrast, tends to have a spot-* ted skin. These sharks can be as long as eleven feet but are not considered dangerous to humans. The long and flexible body allows this shark to push its way in among rocks and *crevices in search of its favorite prey—crabs, shrimps, and small fish. It is found along the tropical coasts of the Indo-Pacific, South Africa, Australia, and Japan.*

96-97 The Port Jackson shark (Heterodontus portusjacksoni) *is of particular interest to researchers, since certain portions of its skeleton are very similar to the skeletons of a long-extinct group that lived in the times of dinosaurs, 100 million years ago.*

The Basking Shark: A Giant in the Sun

The basking shark (Cetorhinus maximus) is a "gentle giant," devoid of teeth, that lives by filtering plankton. It tends to swim just under the surface, its mouth gaping open. The "filter" that captures the minuscule floating animals is contained in the branchial clefts, which can be clearly seen inside this shark's open mouth.

The basking shark is the second largest of all sharks, surpassed in size only by the whale shark. On average, it is about thirty-two feet long, although individuals approaching fifty feet have been reported. This shark feeds only on planktonic crustaceans, cruising on the surface at a speed of about two knots with its mouth open wide, filtering tons of water each hour through its gill rakers. The gill slits of the basking shark are so large they virtually encircle the head. In winter, when the plankton supply is low, the basking shark hibernates on the ocean floor.

It would seem that nature has entrusted the basking shark with the task of ruling over the oceans in areas where the whale shark is not found. The whale shark favors the warm waters of the tropics, while the basking shark travels at higher latitudes. The basking shark is hunted commercially for its enormous, oil-rich liver, which constitutes approximately a quarter of its total body weight.

The basking shark attains sexual maturity around the age of six or seven. The gestation period lasts some three-and-a-half years, and these sharks are reputed to be oophagious, although intrauterine cannibalism is unconfirmed in this species. Young basking sharks bear little resemblance to mature adults, to the extent that for many years, scientists believed that the young of the basking shark were another species entirely. The oversized snout dangles proboscislike over the mouth, the throat curves inward rather than outward with respect to the jaw, and the head is compressed at the sides of the mouth, giving the young shark the appearance of a toothless old elephant with hollow cheeks. Although the snout is less out-of-proportion on adult sharks, because it still somewhat resembles an abbreviated trunk, this shark is known in some parts of the world as the elephant shark.

The crescent-shaped tail, or caudal fin, is quite similar to that of the great white shark and the mako shark; the dorsal fin is "sharkishly" triangular and contains some supporting cartilage, so that rather than cutting through the water as the menacing fins of other sharks do, it gently sways from left to right, as if to signify the docile nature of this giant creature.

This shark swims slowly along near the surface, feeding as it goes and "basking" in the light from above because it so enjoys the warmth of the sun. The basking shark has been observed rolling in the waves belly-up, and it often draws near passing boats and rubs against an oar or allows itself to be scratched with a gaff. It is amusing to speculate that the shark enjoys basking in the sun, but in fact the basking shark indulges in this sort of behavior even when the sky is dark with storm clouds. Gavin Maxwell, an Englishman who for four years following World War II captured basking sharks off the Hebrides, wrote that he was never able to find any satisfactory explanation for this "basking" behavior.

The Megamouth: A Rare and Recent Species

When, in the late 1970s, scientists on board a research vessel off the island of Oahu, Hawaii, found a strange, primitive-looking shark in their nets, they realized immediately that they had discovered an unknown species. The men looked at the fish—a male, over fourteen feet long and weighing over 1,700 pounds—and named it "megamouth." Since the first specimen was discovered, five more have been captured or sighted: three had beached themselves, and two had become tangled in fishermen's nets and were immediately released.

The megamouth shown here—a male, sixteen feet long, with an estimated weight of nearly a ton—was lucky. It was captured by a fishing trawler off Dana Point, California, just after midnight on October 21, 1990. It was immediately returned to the water in the harbor with a line tied to its caudal fin. The following morning, the shark, equipped with a data transmitter, was returned to the open sea, along with an entourage of naturalists and photographers, who took these photographs.

The transmitter provided fifty hours of information about the shark. The megamouth is apparently a "vertical migrator" that spends its daytime hours at depths of up to 500 feet and at nightfall climbs to within 100 feet of the surface.

A curious animal, the megamouth appears to have a tranquil temperament and demonstrates no aggressive tendencies. Like the basking shark, it is a filter-feeder and is not a threat to humans, despite its impressive size.

On these two pages we see the sensational images of the only live megamouth that humans have ever encountered close-up. This very strange shark was first discovered in 1976. Since then, only five others have been found. The most recent specimen to be sighted was found tangled in a trawler's net in October of 1990 near Dana Point, California. On that occasion, the first footage of a live megamouth was taken, along with the photographs shown here. The unfortunate creature had been brought into the harbor by the fishermen, who realized that they had caught something quite unusual. The morning after, the megamouth was taken back out to the open sea, where photographers and researchers had a chance to get close to it, encouraged by the fact that the large and docile shark did not seem to be annoyed or irritated by their presence. This specimen was set free after a small transmitting device was attached to it, making it possible to track the shark's movements and to learn more about its habits, its migratory patterns, and the depths at which it chose to live at different hours of the day and night. It was determined that these sharks vary considerably the depths at which they swim.

The Whale Shark: The Largest Shark in the Sea

Modern sharks first appeared in the Lower Cretaceous period, about 100 million years ago. Their fossilized teeth are virtually identical to those of contemporary sharks. After surviving the extinction of the dinosaurs, sharks spread increasingly throughout the Tertiary Period, maintaining virtually unaltered the same internal physiological structure although decreasing in overall size. The *Carcharodon megalodon*, which has been extinct for twenty million years, had triangular teeth roughly four inches long. A reconstruction of the shark completed by Bashford Dean of the Museum of Natural History in New York in 1909 was significantly oversized: the open mouth was nearly nine feet high. But his data made it possible to establish that the animal was forty-two-and-a-half feet long. Later, other fossil teeth were found that extended roughly six inches, and by extrapolating, it was possible to establish that these teeth belonged to a creature that must have been as large as the largest living creature ever to exist—the great blue whale.

This shark from the distant past seems to have been almost a carbon copy of the great white shark, which today ranks third in terms of size of all the selachians, beaten out only by the whale shark and the basking shark, both of which are easy-going, peaceful plankton feeders. And so, while in distant eras, the largest of sharks was the perhaps most terrifying, death-dealing creature ever to appear on the planet, today the largest of the sharks is the whale shark.

The whale shark has a huge mouth equipped with no fewer than 7,000 teeth, but it has a very small esophagus, is a plankton feeder, and is therefore not considered harmful. The shark's numerous teeth function essentially like the baleen of the great cetaceans, and indeed the whale shark feeds by swimming on or just beneath the surface, allowing its mouth to fill with water that is brimming with plankton or small squid, tiny octopuses, and schools of small fish. The whale shark then closes its enormous jaws and pumps out the water with its tongue, running it through the mesh of the gills, and then gulping down the remaining, living mass. Occasionally, if the whale shark detects a concentration of food below, it will dive, plummeting downward with its jaws agape. At other times, it rises up

TOP LEFT *This view from the top of its tail reveals the distinctive coloring of the whale shark.*

BOTTOM LEFT *The long and almost snakelike body of this whale shark encircles a fascinated diver.*

FACING *One of the many mysteries concerning whale sharks has to do with its remarkable camouflage. The white spots on the shark's back, alternating with pale stripes that are less distinct but perfectly geometric, mimic the effects of sunlight on the water. As a result, the huge fish becomes almost invisible from above. What is not clear is why this fish should "need" to hide; in fact, the whale shark has no predators to fear.*

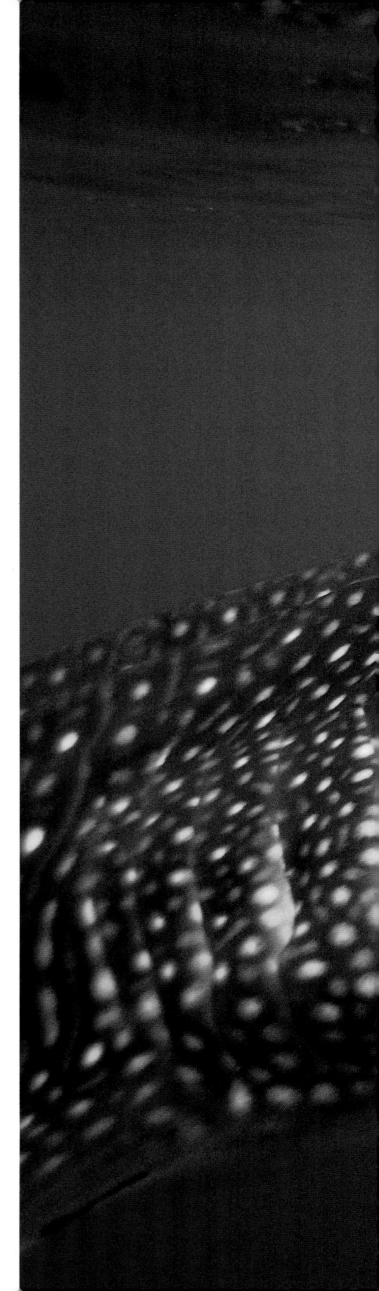

Like basking sharks, whale sharks are filter-feeders, but they appear to do their filter-feeding with greater "initiative." Before opening their mouths, they appear to "aim" at certain zones, which are probably richer in plankton, and they move their heads from side to side so that nothing escapes. Their filtering apparatus is equipped with branchial rakers that appear to have been modified so as to capture and hold huge amounts of food.

106-107 A whale shark is accompanied by a school of remoras. These fish do not always attach themselves to their giant hosts with their suction cups, as the other remoras do, but rather swim alongside.

on its tail a few yards beneath the surface and waits for the food to "drop" into its open mouth.

In Cuba, they call this shark the *Pez dama,* or "checkerboard fish," because of the distinctive pattern on its skin—white on the belly and dark grey or green on the back with intersecting lines or a series of white dots. This creature's silhouette is singular among sharks, with the spine forming a strange hump at the intersection with the pectoral fins. The hump then straightens and the body tapers toward the immense tail, the width of which is nearly equal to a quarter of the shark's length. The belly, too, is unusual for a shark, as it is nearly flat, and the snout has a wide and somewhat flattened shape. The dorsal fin is nearly round and is located much farther back on the shark than it would normally be found. Seen from the front, the whale shark is an odd and impressive creature, with its tiny eyes set low on the colossal head, and the mouth, which is virtually straight across, opening at the tip of the snout rather than in a more ventral position like most other sharks.

In order to survive, a creature of this size requires huge quantities of food. Unlike whales, however, which can safely swim into polar regions where the chilly waters are teeming with krill, the whale shark must make do with what it finds in warm waters. Its range extends 2,400 miles north and south of the equator, with a sharply marked preference for the Philippines, the west coast of Mexico, and, in the Atlantic, the Florida Straits. Although these are its preferred feeding places, it has been sighted both far to the north, off New York, and to the south, off Cape Town in South Africa and Callao in Peru.

At times, this gentle shark takes up residence in a given stretch of water. At the turn of the century, there was one whale shark that, after shuttling for a while between Cuba and Santo Domingo, decided to stay just off San Juan, Puerto Rico, and remained for a year. Another whale shark set up house near Yucatan, in Mexico, where he was named "Big Ben." Yet another was dubbed "Sapodilla Tom" for his extended stay in Sapodilla Bay in British Honduras. The most recent reports of a resident whale shark came from Cojimar, Cuba, where the fishermen called him "El Elefante."

Marine giants often prove friendly and inquisitive toward humans, allowing them to approach and at times even to ride on their backs. Sometimes they are the first to demonstrate openness and friendliness when they encounter scuba divers. In the Indian Ocean, natives tell of small accidents with whale sharks, in which an occasional canoe has been overturned. In all likelihood, however, the whale shark simply failed to notice these boats in the water.

As in the basking shark, in the whale shark the filtering apparatus is found at the level of the gills.

110-111 Whale sharks can be found mainly in tropical waters; in particular, they seek out areas rich in plankton, which often coincide with areas in which warm waters mix with cold.

An Introduction to Sharks

Maddalena Jahoda

From an evolutionary point of view, sharks constitute a spectacular success story: the fossil record dates back over 300 million years and predates that of the dinosaurs. These predators have always had a remarkable ability to adapt to their environment. There are no herbivorous sharks; all sharks prey on other living things. This does not mean that all sharks are dangerous, like the great white or the tiger shark. Indeed, many species are quite harmless. Some sharks do no more "damage" than cracking the shells of mollusks or nipping at small fish, and others merely filter plankton from the water they swim through.

Sharks are often classified as "primitive" creatures; their cartilaginous skeletons are considered to be precursors to the bones found in most other types of fish. This does not mean, however, that sharks are not highly specialized; some experts believe that sharks' bones may have lost their capacity to calcify as a form of adaptation. Another feature that distinguishes sharks from bony fish is their skin, which is covered with denticles rather than scales.

The great evolutionary success of sharks is attributable to their ability to adapt to a wide range of environments; there isn't an ocean, fjord, or coral reef that is off-limits— from shallow coastal waters to the deepest abyss. The bull shark can actually be found in fresh water, since it swims up rivers and has been known to inhabit lakes, such as Lake Nicaragua and Lake Izbal in Guatemala.

No one knows for certain how many species of sharks exist. There are an estimated 350 species in some 30 families, which are in turn grouped into a dozen or so orders. Sharks are part of the group Chondrichthyes—cartilaginous fish— which also includes stingrays, manta rays, and skates, among others. In fact, the other members of this group are compressed or "flattened" shark derivatives that have adapted for life on the bottom of the sea.

Many well-known sharks belong to the order Lamniformes, or mackerel sharks. These include the great white, the mako, the sand tiger, the basking shark, and the megamouth. Requiem sharks, catsharks, and hammerheads belong to the order Carcharhiniformes, or groundsharks. The whale shark and

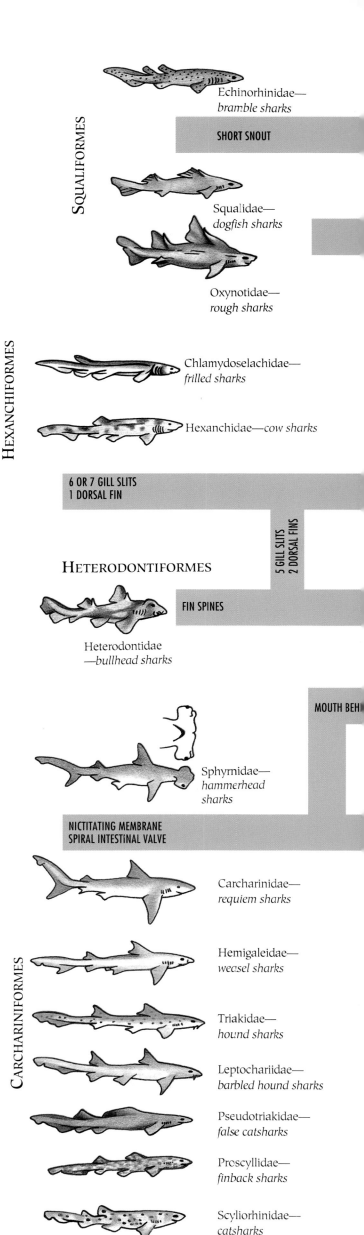

SQUALIFORMES

Echinorhinidae— *bramble sharks*

SHORT SNOUT

Squalidae— *dogfish sharks*

Oxynotidae— *rough sharks*

HEXANCHIFORMES

Chlamydoselachidae— *frilled sharks*

Hexanchidae—*cow sharks*

6 OR 7 GILL SLITS 1 DORSAL FIN

5 GILL SLITS 2 DORSAL FINS

HETERODONTIFORMES

FIN SPINES

Heterodontidae —*bullhead sharks*

MOUTH BEH

Sphyrnidae— *hammerhead sharks*

NICTITATING MEMBRANE SPIRAL INTESTINAL VALVE

CARCHARINIFORMES

Carcharinidae— *requiem sharks*

Hemigaleidae— *weasel sharks*

Triakidae— *hound sharks*

Leptochariidae— *barbled hound sharks*

Pseudotriakidae— *false catsharks*

Proscyllidae— *finback sharks*

Scyliorhinidae— *catsharks*

saw sharks

ELONGATED SNOUT

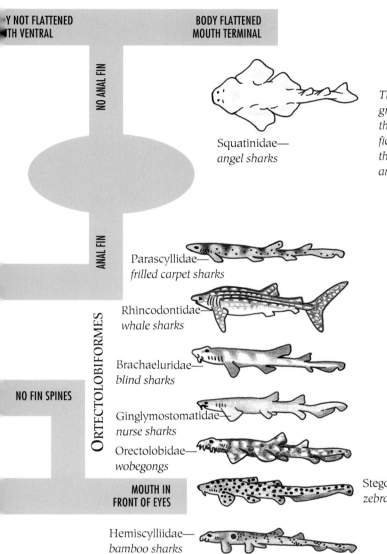

Y NOT FLATTENED
TH VENTRAL

BODY FLATTENED
MOUTH TERMINAL

NO ANAL FIN

ANAL FIN

ORECTOLOBIFORMES

NO FIN SPINES

Squatinidae—
angel sharks

Parascyllidae—
frilled carpet sharks

Rhincodontidae—
whale sharks

Brachaeluridae—
blind sharks

Ginglymostomatidae—
nurse sharks

Orectolobidae—
wobegongs

Stegostomatidae—
zebra sharks

MOUTH IN
FRONT OF EYES

Hemiscylliidae—
bamboo sharks

This illustration shows the main groups of sharks according to the most widely accepted classifications— those developed by the scholar L. J. V. Compagno, among others.

NO NICTITATING MEMBRANE
RING INTESTINAL VALVE

LAMNIFORMES
Lamnidae—
true mackerel sharks

Alopiidae—
thresher sharks

Cetorhinidae—
basking sharks

Megachasmidae—
megamouths

Mitsukurinidae—
goblin sharks

Pseudocarchariidae—
crocodile sharks

Odontaspidae—
sand tiger sharks

the nurse shark belong to the order Orectolobiformes, or carpetsharks. In addition to these, there are at least six other orders.

How did sharks evolve? The history of a group of animals is always challenging to reconstruct, but in this case, the difficulties are particularly daunting. Indeed, it is possible for species with bones to be preserved in the form of fossils, but all that remains of sharks, in the best cases, are their teeth. The oldest shark known to man, the Cladoselache, constitutes an exception to this rule, because it was very well preserved when it was found on the shores of Lake Erie. It dates from 300 million years ago, and its

ancestors probably broke off from the bony fish about 400 million years ago. The Cladoselache lived in the Devonian Period. Dinosaurs did not appear for another hundred million years.

But if we are looking for "modern" sharks, then we must wait for the period ranging from 100 million to 70 million years ago, which is to say the time when the giant reptiles were already becoming extinct and mammals were timidly making their first appearance. At that time, most of the genera we know today already existed: the sand tiger shark, the basking shark, the nurse shark, the tiger shark, catsharks, and the Carcharhinidae.

But the most fearsome carnivore the world has ever known dates from 50 million years ago: this was the *Carchardon megaladon*, similar to the modern-day great white shark but much bigger. From the size of its teeth, which were nearly twice the size of those of the great white, it has been calculated that its mouth must have opened to a width of six-and-a-half feet. The shark must have been nearly forty-three feet in length (early estimates of ninety-eight feet were probably wrong). This shark survived for 15 million years until, for reasons unknown to us, it died out.

But such was not the case for other "ancient" species. In 1889, a shark with a bizarre shape was found, with an odd protuberance in its forehead—a fish that had never been reported before. It was named the goblin shark, although not for long. Scientists soon realized, from a dental comparison, that this was a Scapanorhynchus—a species that had been believed to be extinct for 100 million years.

Great white shark

Carcharodon carcharias

Average length: 460 cm

Distribution: temperate and subtropical
  coastal waters

The most feared but also the most studied of all sharks—the great white— ranks highest in number of attacks on humans. One of the largest known specimens of a great white tipped the scales at just over two tons and measured almost twenty-one feet in length.

The great white shark is not precisely the color that is indicated by its name; it has rather a greyish or brownish color on its back and a beige or cream color on the belly. Often it has a black splotch where its pectoral flipper juts out. The species can most easily be identified by its characteristic triangular teeth with serrated edges. The pupils of the great white's eyes are round and black. The tail is more symmetrical than in most other sharks, with the upper and lower lobes nearly equal in size.

Although these sharks are generally not found in water any shallower than about ninety-eight feet, their distribution tends to follow the coastlines. In areas where the depth drops gradually, these sharks tend to swim farther out to sea, while in areas where the continental shelf drops away suddenly, such as along the Pacific coast of the United States, these sharks tend to come in closer to land.

Among the specific adaptations that have made the great white shark such a dangerous predator is its ability to keep its body temperature up to ten degrees higher than the surrounding water temperature. This makes its muscles more efficient. The great white can feed on just about any prey it likes among the larger fish, including other sharks, as well as marine mammals such as dolphins and seals.

Strong, fast, tenacious, and aggressive when it attacks, the great white is considered to be the most unpredictable of sharks. Unlike other species, such as the tiger and the mako, which generally swim around their victims before deciding to attack, the great white shark skips all preambles and takes its victim immediately. On the other hand, some great whites have been observed to flee at the first contact with divers.

Man-eaters

Bees are far more dangerous than sharks. (More people die each year from beestings than from shark bites.) And yet for a great many people, the great white shark is the very embodiment of terror. Rivers of words have been poured forth in efforts to explain why great white sharks attack humans, but the findings have often been quite disappointing. And there are a great many experts who have had to confess that the best system for protecting oneself from a shark attack is just to stay out of the water.

Attempts have been made, from time to time, to correlate shark attacks with other "predictable" elements. Many factors have been taken into consideration, including the murkiness, temperature, salinity, and depth of the water; the distance from the coast; weather condi-

These pictures show the protruding action involved in the sequence of a bite by a great white.

tions; the color of the victim's bathing suit; the color of the victim's skin; the presence or absence of jewelry; the time of the attack; the season; the state of the tides; and so on. The interpretation of the findings has not always been satisfactory. For instance, it seemed at one point that the attacks always took place in less than six feet of water, and so one might have understandably presumed that it was safer to swim in deeper waters. Employing similar criteria, someone else advanced the "warm water" theory, according to which sharks would only attack when the temperature of the water was above twelve degrees Celsius. In reality, however, there was another explanation in both cases: there are more people swimming in shallow water than in deep, and likewise, more bathers are found in warm water than in cold.

One of the most laudable efforts to gather systematically detailed information concerning shark attacks was done by a group of experts who compiled a body of information called the Shark Attack File, an international data bank on attacks, organized by an ichthyologist at the Smithsonian Institution in Washington, D.C. In fourteen years, information was assembled concerning 1,652 confirmed cases.

What emerged was a ranking of the most "murderous" sharks. They are (in order): the great white, the mako, the bull shark, the hammerhead, and the great blue shark. Another ranking includes the most dangerous coastlines: Australia, eastern North America, Africa, western North America, and Asia. Other information listed concerns which parts of the body are bitten most often (legs below the knee, thighs, arms, feet, hands, and sides), the number of bites inflicted per attack (most often, three), and lastly, the location of the victim in the water (the majority were swimming on the surface, as opposed to diving).

Further efforts by the researchers working on the problem of sharks (often on behalf of the American Navy, which was concerned about sailors shipwrecked during wartime) led to some progress. It would seem, for instance, that quite often sharks set to work to savage one victim only, even when there might be a number of people floating on the surface; thus it has happened that rescuers have literally pulled a person from the jaws of a shark without being attacked themselves. The reason is that a "swarm" of potential victims tends to disorient a predator, for if the predator chooses to snap at random in a crowd, it will probably not get very much for its trouble. Perhaps that is why the shark tends to set its sights on a specific individual, ignoring others even if they are easily available. Surfers, who generally paddle their way out to sea while lying face-down on their surfboards, are perhaps treated no differently than other prey. To a great white, in fact, the silhouette of a paddling surfer as seen from below—something that is compact and tapered with four appendages

The graphs below show the percentage of attacks on the various days of the week and at various times of the day.

Over the years, numerous efforts have been made to correlate shark attacks on humans with many external factors; we've listed times, dates, and types of attacks. We do not yet have any satisfactory results; *basically, it has been possible to establish that attacks are more frequent when there are many bathers in the water, and therefore chiefly during the weekend, during holidays, and immediately before and after* *midday. This obviously does not mean that sharks are "hungrier" on the weekend or at certain times of the day, but rather that there are greater opportunities for attacks the more people there are in the water.*

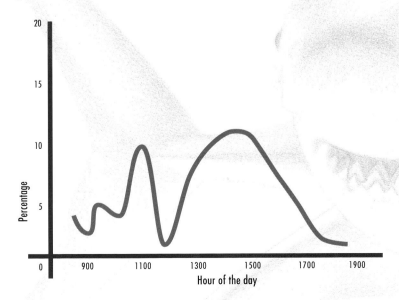

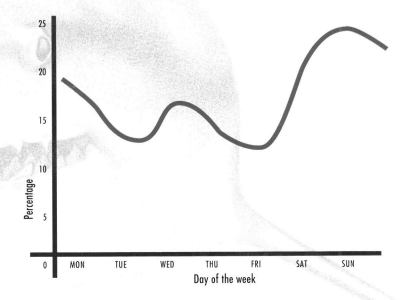

Tiger shark

Galeocerdo cuvier

Length: 330-420 cm

Distribution: temperate and tropical
waters around the world

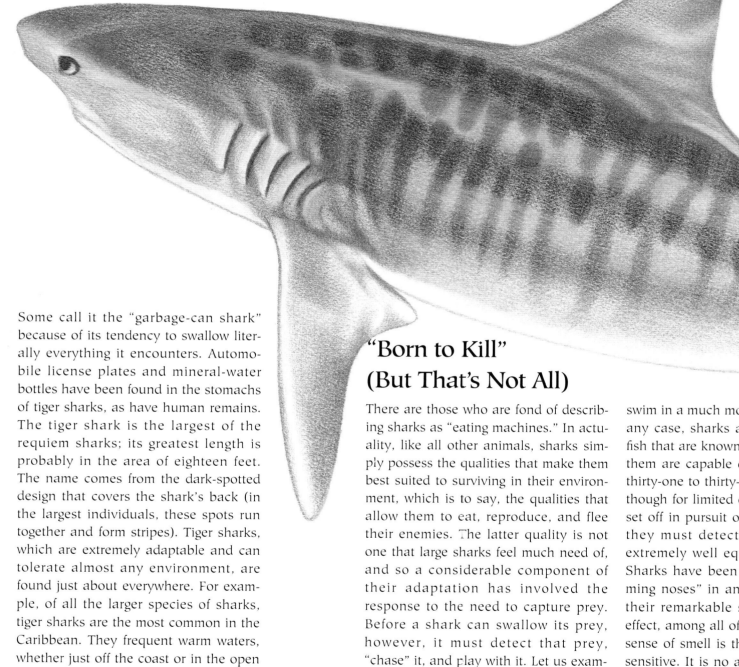

Some call it the "garbage-can shark"
because of its tendency to swallow literally everything it encounters. Automo-
bile license plates and mineral-water
bottles have been found in the stomachs
of tiger sharks, as have human remains.
The tiger shark is the largest of the
requiem sharks; its greatest length is
probably in the area of eighteen feet.
The name comes from the dark-spotted
design that covers the shark's back (in
the largest individuals, these spots run
together and form stripes). Tiger sharks,
which are extremely adaptable and can
tolerate almost any environment, are
found just about everywhere. For example, of all the larger species of sharks,
tiger sharks are the most common in the
Caribbean. They frequent warm waters,
whether just off the coast or in the open
sea, but it is not uncommon for them to
suddenly appear in "new" stalking
grounds. They tend to be active at night,
and when night falls they draw quite
close to the coasts, swimming even in
very shallow water. Normally a tiger
shark gives one the impression of being
a fairly "lazy" swimmer, but when it
scents food, it becomes quite active. The
tiger shark is considered to be one of the
species most dangerous to man.

"Born to Kill" (But That's Not All)

There are those who are fond of describ-
ing sharks as "eating machines." In actu-
ality, like all other animals, sharks simply possess the qualities that make them
best suited to surviving in their environment, which is to say, the qualities that
allow them to eat, reproduce, and flee
their enemies. The latter quality is not
one that large sharks feel much need of,
and so a considerable component of
their adaptation has involved the
response to the need to capture prey.
Before a shark can swallow its prey,
however, it must detect that prey,
"chase" it, and play with it. Let us exam-
ine some of the sophisticated systems
that sharks have developed in order to
attain these goals.

While the pectoral fins are used as
tillers, the chief mode of propulsion
involves the powerful thrusts of the tail,
which, in many species, has an upper
lobe that is more developed than the
lower one. Some species move forward
through the water by using thrusts of the
tail while holding the body rigid; others

swim in a much more flexible manner. In
any case, sharks are among the fastest
fish that are known to man, and many of
them are capable of attaining speeds of
thirty-one to thirty-seven miles per hour,
though for limited distances. Before they
set off in pursuit of their prey, however,
they must detect it—and sharks are
extremely well equipped for this task.
Sharks have been described as "swimming noses" in an effort to underscore
their remarkable sensory capacity. In
effect, among all of a shark's senses, the
sense of smell is the most powerful and
sensitive. It is no accident that olfactory
lobes occupy a good part of the brain.

Contrary to popular belief, a
shark's sense of sight is fairly good, even
though light penetrates only a few dozen
yards in water. In order to make the best
possible use of the limited amount of
light that is available, there are special
"devices," including the presence, in the
shark's eye, of a sort of mirror, or "carpet" of reflecting cells. As for the pupil, it
is smaller or larger depending on

Tiger shark

Galeocerdo cuvier

Length: 330-420 cm

Distribution: temperate and tropical
waters around the world

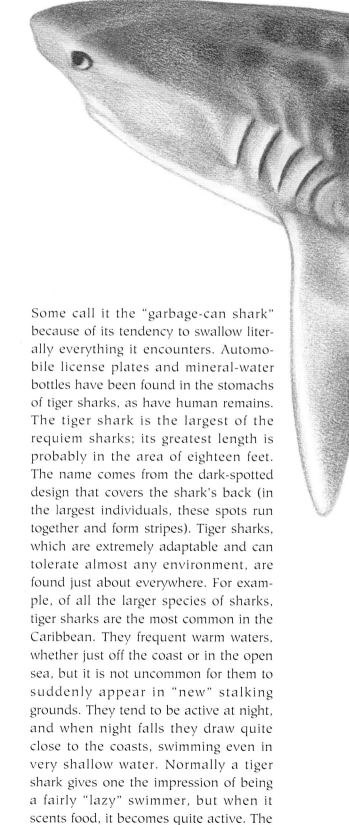

Some call it the "garbage-can shark"
because of its tendency to swallow literally everything it encounters. Automo-
bile license plates and mineral-water
bottles have been found in the stomachs
of tiger sharks, as have human remains.
The tiger shark is the largest of the
requiem sharks; its greatest length is
probably in the area of eighteen feet.
The name comes from the dark-spotted
design that covers the shark's back (in
the largest individuals, these spots run
together and form stripes). Tiger sharks,
which are extremely adaptable and can
tolerate almost any environment, are
found just about everywhere. For example, of all the larger species of sharks,
tiger sharks are the most common in the
Caribbean. They frequent warm waters,
whether just off the coast or in the open
sea, but it is not uncommon for them to
suddenly appear in "new" stalking
grounds. They tend to be active at night,
and when night falls they draw quite
close to the coasts, swimming even in
very shallow water. Normally a tiger
shark gives one the impression of being
a fairly "lazy" swimmer, but when it
scents food, it becomes quite active. The
tiger shark is considered to be one of the
species most dangerous to man.

"Born to Kill" (But That's Not All)

There are those who are fond of describ-
ing sharks as "eating machines." In actu-
ality, like all other animals, sharks simply possess the qualities that make them
best suited to surviving in their environment, which is to say, the qualities that
allow them to eat, reproduce, and flee
their enemies. The latter quality is not
one that large sharks feel much need of,
and so a considerable component of
their adaptation has involved the
response to the need to capture prey.
Before a shark can swallow its prey,
however, it must detect that prey,
"chase" it, and play with it. Let us exam-
ine some of the sophisticated systems
that sharks have developed in order to
attain these goals.

While the pectoral fins are used as
tillers, the chief mode of propulsion
involves the powerful thrusts of the tail,
which, in many species, has an upper
lobe that is more developed than the
lower one. Some species move forward
through the water by using thrusts of the
tail while holding the body rigid; others

swim in a much more flexible manner. In
any case, sharks are among the fastest
fish that are known to man, and many of
them are capable of attaining speeds of
thirty-one to thirty-seven miles per hour,
though for limited distances. Before they
set off in pursuit of their prey, however,
they must detect it—and sharks are
extremely well equipped for this task.
Sharks have been described as "swimming noses" in an effort to underscore
their remarkable sensory capacity. In
effect, among all of a shark's senses, the
sense of smell is the most powerful and
sensitive. It is no accident that olfactory
lobes occupy a good part of the brain.

Contrary to popular belief, a
shark's sense of sight is fairly good, even
though light penetrates only a few dozen
yards in water. In order to make the best
possible use of the limited amount of
light that is available, there are special
"devices," including the presence, in the
shark's eye, of a sort of mirror, or "carpet" of reflecting cells. As for the pupil, it
is smaller or larger depending on

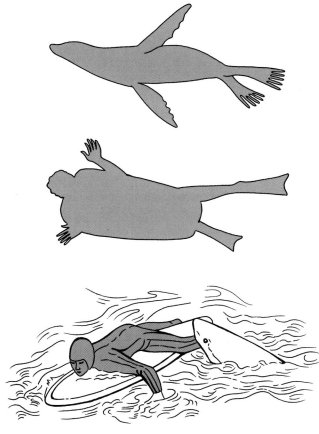

Attacks

The silhouette of a man lying on a surfboard (in this case, also wearing flippers) is very similar to the silhouette of a pinniped, and in particular, to that of an otter—a favorite prey of sharks. This is probably the reason why surfers are the category of bathers most likely to fall victim to shark attacks.

A number of factors are cited in support of this theory, which could be called the "non-man-eater theory": first, that out of all of the various attacks that have occurred, little more than a third have proved fatal. Moreover, the victim often dies from causes such as loss of blood, organ damage, or shock, and not because the shark eats him or her. As for the human limbs that have been found in the stomachs of sharks, it has often been impossible to demonstrate that they were the result of an attack on a living human being; in fact, it is quite possible that the shark had simply gulped down parts of a corpse it had found quite by accident. And sharks do have a certain learning capacity—especially where food is concerned. If it were to prove true that they could become "accustomed" to the taste of human flesh, then they would certainly line up along the beaches in the summer, just as they line up behind ships that dump garbage in the ocean.

An entirely separate case, however, is that of shipwrecked sailors such as those who were killed by sharks during World War II. In such instances, all of the features that can attract sharks are combined—there are a great number of humans in the water; there is the constant flapping about of arms and legs, often amid shrieks and cries, and a copious loss of blood. Several such incidents during World War II showed dramatically that in these situations, sharks do actually devour human beings. As for blood, it has been said that a single drop is enough to set off a feeding frenzy.

Even if it is true that sharks have a remarkable olfactory sense and that experiments under controlled conditions have shown that they demonstrate a certain "preference" for human blood, it is also true that there have been cases in which attack victims have been released immediately by the shark, even while they were still bleeding copiously. And, even in these cases, other sharks were not always attracted, nor did the much-feared feeding frenzy necessarily ensue in every case. This disturbing phenomenon, in which the sharks become so excited that they even begin savaging and mauling one another, may not necessarily be a natural form of behavior; it could well be a reaction to a situation created by humans. Indeed, feeding frenzies typically occur when a huge amount of food is tossed into the water as bait.

This map shows the distribution of attacks made by different species of sharks against humans. Certain areas are more often the site of attacks than others; such is the case in Natal, in southern Africa, for example, and the east coasts of Australia and the United States, and the California coast. One cannot safely say, however, that these statistics truly reflect the actual situation, inasmuch as they rely on the reporting that is done, with greater or lesser accuracy, in the various zones.

The color red indicates the zones where more than 100 attacks have been reported, green represents from 50 to 100 attacks, yellow indicates from 30 to 50 attacks, black from 10 to 30 attacks, and orange represents from 1 to 10.

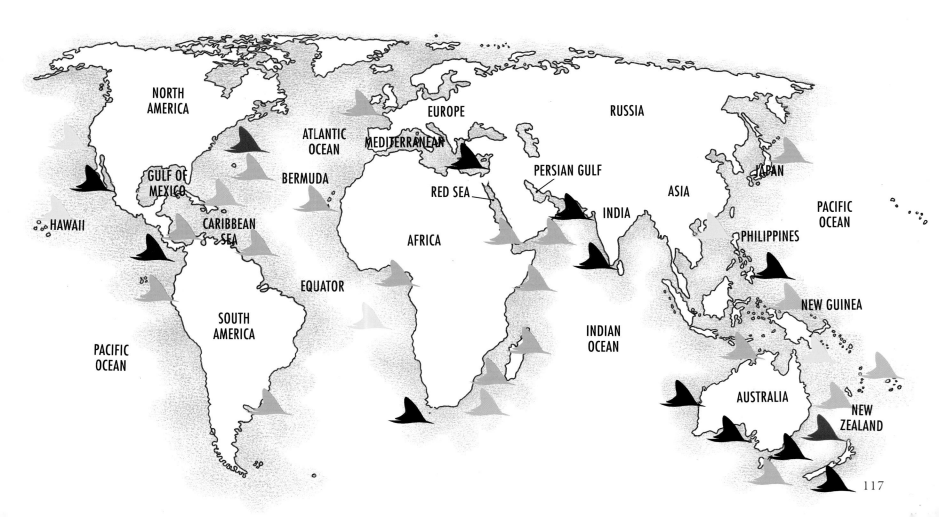

117

Sight

In contrast to what people have long believed, sharks have a well-developed sense of sight. The retina is equipped with rods and cones. Behind the retina, there are special reflective plates that form a layer called the "tapetum lucidum." Their job is to intensify the images perceived, allowing the shark to see even when the light is very dim. In some species of shark, the eyes are protected by movable membranes called nictitating membranes, which serve to cover and protect the eye when the shark attacks.

Inner ear

Hearing is also well developed in sharks and does more than merely perceive sounds—it also provides balance and a sense of direction. The inner ear is closely connected with the lateral line. Enclosed in the cranium, the inner ear is supplied with groups of ciliate cells that are sensitive to vibrations at frequencies less than a thousand cycles per second. This great acoustic sensitivity, combined with the other senses, allows sharks to detect even the slightest variations in sound produced at enormous distances. Sharks are thus aware of everything going on around them for a considerable distance.

Lateral line

The lateral line is a complex sensory organ that runs the length of the shark's body on both sides, starting from the eye and reaching all the way to the tip of the tail. It is made up of ciliate cells that are sensitive to low-frequency pressure waves, which the normal ear cannot perceive. This makes it possible for the shark to detect vibrations emitted by animals that are either wounded or engaged in a struggle, even at a considerable distance. The stimuli that reach the lateral line convey to the brain the required information for the shark to track down the prey and capture it.

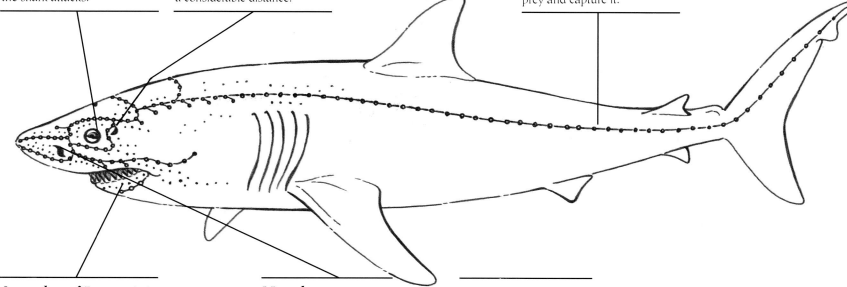

Ampules of Lorenzini

The ampules of Lorenzini are special sensory organs linked to the pores of the shark's skin through long canals. The ampules of Lorenzini are capable of transmitting to the brain indicators of even extremely weak electrical fields, thus increasing to a remarkable degree the ability of the shark to capture its prey.

Nasal sacs

The principal source of chemical sensitivity, the sense of smell, is seated in the olfactory sacs in the shark. These are spiral-shaped membranes located on the interior of the shark's nares. Sharks have an extremely acute sense of smell, and it involves a considerable portion of the brain's functions. A number of experiments have been performed in this context to find repellent substances that tend to disturb or chase away sharks. Moreover, it has been discovered that the chemical components of flesh and blood are detected by sharks even at very low concentrations.

---

sticking out—looks remarkably like the outline of a seal or an otter and is therefore often considered to be something that will be good to eat.

Less easy to interpret is the fact that some 93 percent of all attack victims were male; only 85 cases out of 1,162 involved women. There are a number of possible explanations. At the time the data were gathered for the Shark Attack File (between 1958 and 1972), it could be that more men went swimming than women, or it could be that men are stronger and more aggressive swimmers than women (vigorous movement attracts sharks), or perhaps men taste or smell different from women.

Likewise, in an effort to establish some rules, someone suggested that sharks could be provoked to attack when a person plunged suddenly into the water: diving or falling from a boat could seem like threatening, aggressive actions to a shark. This is an idea no more persuasive or powerful than any other, but it does introduce a new concept—that perhaps sharks do not necessarily attack for food. It had always been taken for granted that sharks attacked humans out of hunger, and thus the legend sprang up that once a shark had tasted human flesh, it would then return in search of more.

Today, however, we tend to interpret the behavior of sharks in quite a different way. Some experts maintain that many shark attacks are simply the unfortunate outcome of an effort to identify the nature of a potential prey. An Australian diver, Rodney Fox, received a bite to his side, just below the shoulder; if the great white that attacked him while he was scuba diving had wanted to, it could have snapped Fox in two. And so it may be that the shark was just nibbling at something it thought might be good to eat and let Fox go as soon as it realized that he was something else entirely. This reflects what is believed to be the "psychology" of a large shark: everything that moves might be good to eat, and the best way to tell if something is edible is . . . to bite it.

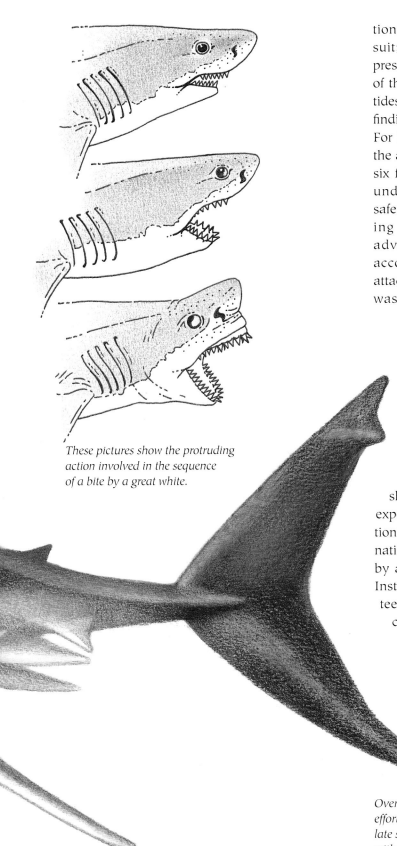

These pictures show the protruding action involved in the sequence of a bite by a great white.

tions; the color of the victim's bathing suit; the color of the victim's skin; the presence or absence of jewelry; the time of the attack; the season; the state of the tides; and so on. The interpretation of the findings has not always been satisfactory. For instance, it seemed at one point that the attacks always took place in less than six feet of water, and so one might have understandably presumed that it was safer to swim in deeper waters. Employing similar criteria, someone else advanced the "warm water" theory, according to which sharks would only attack when the temperature of the water was above twelve degrees Celsius. In reality, however, there was another explanation in both cases: there are more people swimming in shallow water than in deep, and likewise, more bathers are found in warm water than in cold.

One of the most laudable efforts to gather systematically detailed information concerning shark attacks was done by a group of experts who compiled a body of information called the Shark Attack File, an international data bank on attacks, organized by an ichthyologist at the Smithsonian Institution in Washington, D.C. In fourteen years, information was assembled concerning 1,652 confirmed cases.

What emerged was a ranking of the most "murderous" sharks. They are (in order): the great white, the mako, the bull shark, the hammerhead, and the great blue shark. Another ranking includes the most dangerous coastlines: Australia, eastern North America, Africa, western North America, and Asia. Other information listed concerns which parts of the body are bitten most often (legs below the knee, thighs, arms, feet, hands, and sides), the number of bites inflicted per attack (most often, three), and lastly, the location of the victim in the water (the majority were swimming on the surface, as opposed to diving).

Further efforts by the researchers working on the problem of sharks (often on behalf of the American Navy, which was concerned about sailors shipwrecked during wartime) led to some progress. It would seem, for instance, that quite often sharks set to work to savage one victim only, even when there might be a number of people floating on the surface; thus it has happened that rescuers have literally pulled a person from the jaws of a shark without being attacked themselves. The reason is that a "swarm" of potential victims tends to disorient a predator, for if the predator chooses to snap at random in a crowd, it will probably not get very much for its trouble. Perhaps that is why the shark tends to set its sights on a specific individual, ignoring others even if they are easily available. Surfers, who generally paddle their way out to sea while lying face-down on their surfboards, are perhaps treated no differently than other prey. To a great white, in fact, the silhouette of a paddling surfer as seen from below—something that is compact and tapered with four appendages

Over the years, numerous efforts have been made to correlate shark attacks on humans with many external factors; we've listed times, dates, and types of attacks. We do not yet have any satisfactory results; basically, it has been possible to establish that attacks are more frequent when there are many bathers in the water, and therefore chiefly during the weekend, during holidays, and immediately before and after midday. This obviously does not mean that sharks are "hungrier" on the weekend or at certain times of the day, but rather that there are greater opportunities for attacks the more people there are in the water.

The graphs below show the percentage of attacks on the various days of the week and at various times of the day.

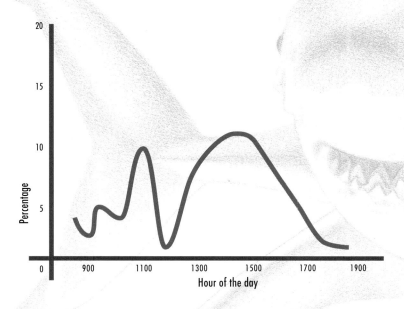

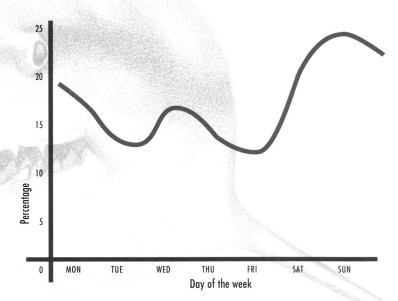

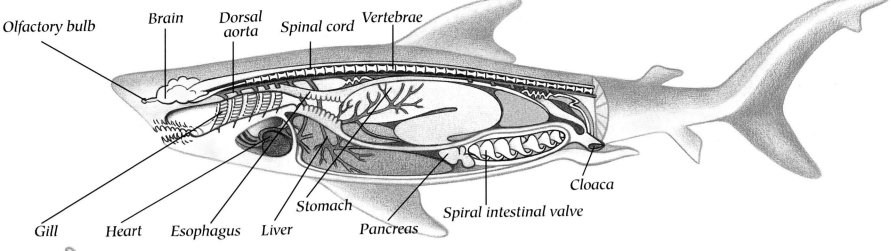

Olfactory bulb   Brain   Dorsal aorta   Spinal cord   Vertebrae

Cloaca

Gill   Heart   Esophagus   Liver   Stomach   Pancreas   Spiral intestinal valve

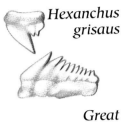

Hexanchus grisaus

Great white shark

Tiger shark

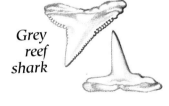

Grey reef shark

Sand tiger shark

Nurse shark

whether the species lives near the surface or in the deep, but the distinctive "icy gaze" of the shark results from the fact that the eye can only close for an instant at a time, through the nictitating membrane; this is a third eyelid which, in certain species, temporarily covers the eye when it needs protection—for instance, when the shark attacks.

Prey that the shark may not be able to see because it is too far away, the shark can feel, through a system of lateral mechanoreceptors (a series of channels filled with fluid) that run along the shark's flank. Through these, the shark can perceive both acoustical waves and pressure waves. Thus, it can not only hear sounds, but it can also detect movements. Sharks can, in this manner, detect vibrations from as far as 650 feet away.

The set of sensory organs a shark relies on for hunting is completed by the sense of taste (which is pretty well developed), the sense of touch (which, on the other hand, is limited), and the electroreceptors.

A great deal has been written about sharks' teeth—indeed, they are razor-sharp and awe-inspiring weapons. Unlike human teeth, the teeth of sharks are not set into the bone, but rather they are set into the soft tissue inside the mouth. They grow in successive rows that move gradually toward the exterior. The result is that at any given time, only one row of teeth is actually "function-

ing," but as soon as the teeth in that row are damaged or worn down, the next line is ready to take its place. In certain cases, a set of teeth is replaced every week, and in the space of ten years, a shark might make use of some 20,000 teeth.

But the shark's teeth are not found only in the shark's mouth; sharks are literally covered with "teeth," though of a different sort. The distinctive roughness of the skin of a shark results from the fact that the skin is covered with an endless array of dermal denticles, also known as placoid scales. The structure is not unlike that of real teeth, with a central "pulp" and a dentin outer covering. Each dermal denticle has a tip that points backward, so the sharkskin feels smooth if rubbed in one direction (from front to back) and rough if rubbed in the opposite direction. The only exception to this rule occurs in basking sharks, whose dermal denticles are omnidirectional. In some cases, it has been possible to identify the actual shark that bit an object by the teeth the shark left embedded in it. And that's not all: even the dermal denticles of the various species are distinctive, though they may vary from one part of the body to another, and they can also be used in identifying the shark. In any case, these dermal denticles form an armor that is in itself quite dangerous: if a swimmer is even bumped by a shark, serious abrasions may result.

Skin and denticles

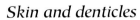

The distinctive roughness of the skin of sharks is caused by the dermal denticles. These cover the entire surface of the body and are arranged in such a way as to channel the water, reducing friction to a minimum in swimming. In the illustration at top, the denticles of the whale shark are shown, and at bottom, the denticles of the grey shark.

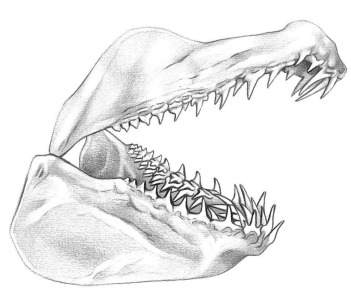

Teeth

The teeth are distinctive in the various species to the point that it is possible to identify the shark that made a bite mark simply by matching the bite to the teeth. The shape of the teeth varies according to the function those teeth are meant

to perform, and, more precisely, according to the different prey these sharks consume. Arranged in numerous rows, the teeth are periodically replaced by new ones, which "migrate" from the interior of the mouth to the exterior.

Sand tiger shark

Carcharias taurus

Length: 220-300 cm

Distribution: temperate and tropical
coastal waters around the world

What one notices first about these
sharks are the amazing rows of sharp,
jagged teeth that tend to protrude from
the mouth. In reality, these teeth are
fairly small and are used not for ripping
mouthfuls of flesh from larger prey but
for seizing fish, which the shark then
swallows whole. The two dorsal fins,
each the same size, are also fairly distinctive. The sand tiger shark is generally found in shallow water (down to 650
feet) not too far from the coast. It
swims in a manner that cannot be
described as particularly vigorous, and
it is especially active at night. By day, it
can be observed lying motionless on
the sea floor.

The sand tiger shark is not considered to be particularly dangerous to
humans, and indeed there are no reports
of unprovoked attacks, but it may react
if provoked. Some of the attacks that
have been attributed to sand tiger sharks
in Australia are probably the handiwork
of other species. The relatively peaceful
temperament of the adult sand tiger
shark differs significantly from that of
the sand tiger shark fetus, which
engages in intrauterine cannibalism,
feeding on its smaller siblings while still
in the womb. For this reason, these
sharks give birth to no more than two
young at a time, one for each uterus.

Shark Reproduction

Stewart Springer was an American
zoologist who held an unusual distinction: he may have been the only person
to have been bitten by an as-yet-unborn
shark. This unpleasant experience,
which took place while he was dissecting
a female sand tiger shark, led him to
begin a new field of research—into what
has come to be known as intrauterine
cannibalism—one of the many oddities
surrounding the reproduction of sharks.

The topic of shark reproduction is
often confusing, because we speak, on
the one hand, about the laying of eggs,
and on the other, about live birth. In
reality, not only do sharks have different
ways of reproducing, but some species
also have actually "invented" a method
that is surprisingly similar to that used
by mammals.

Often, the moment of coupling is
the only time that one shark will have
anything at all to do with another member of its species. And this does not really qualify as a tender moment, since in

order to convince the female to assume
the appropriate position, the male has to
bite her repeatedly. In truth, quite often
both male and female sharks often
emerge from the act of mating in worse
shape than they went into it, with bites
and cuts all over their bodies. In order to
prevent significant damage, however,
females are endowed with a particularly
thick skin.

Male sharks are easily recognized
by their claspers—two cylindrical off-
shoots of the pelvic fins supported by
bits of calcified cartilage. Normally,
these claspers face backward, in line
with the shark's body, but they are rotat-
ed forward when the time comes to
mate, so that each fin depresses a
siphon—a subcutaneous pocket that fills
with water. As soon as one of the
claspers is introduced into the cloaca of
the female, the water in the siphon is
expelled, along with the shark's sperm.
Following fertilization, each species
implements its own "technique" of

reproduction. The term "oviparous" applies when the young sharks grow in an egg that is then placed in an outside environment, "viviparous" when the young emerge from the mother's body fully formed, "ovoviviparous" when eggs are produced but then hatch inside the mother's body.

Sharks that are born directly from eggs include the catsharks and the sharks that belong to the family Heterodontidae. Catsharks produce a distinctive transparent casing that "houses" the young shark during the period of gestation. In particular the Heterodontus, or bullhead sharks (small, sea-bed dwellers), lay a very strange egg indeed; it is a spiral-shaped egg that is literally screwed into cracks in the rock, from which, once it hardens, it cannot easily be freed.

But the most common system of reproduction among sharks is the "viviparous"; this method has been adopted by more than forty of the fifty shark families known to science. In this category, zoologists today tend to group the "ovoviviparous" sharks as well, since the distinction between the two categories is fairly vague. The difference is largely a matter of whether or not the fetus receives nourishment from the mother. There are plenty of case studies available, since the range goes from the young that live inside their mothers' bodies, living on the yolks of their own eggs, to the intrauterine cannibals mentioned above, to those young sharks which, once they have finished the yolks of their own eggs, wait for the arrival of other eggs produced by their mothers. In viviparous species, such as members of the Carcharhinidae, the fertilized egg resides in the oviduct within uterine compartments for a considerable period of time (ranging from nine months to two years). Unlike mammals, sharks do not take care of their young. Newborn sharks are abandoned and must fend for themselves—something they are eminently equipped to do—as sharks are born ready and able to lead the life of a predator.

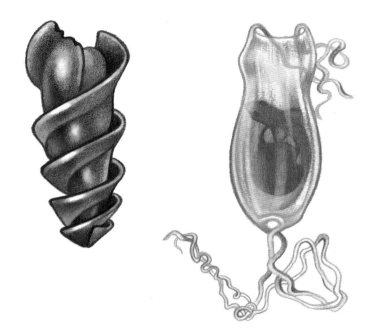

A number of species reproduce by laying eggs. On the left, the remarkable egg of Heterodontus, a small, bottom-dwelling shark, is shown. The egg is spiral-shaped, and it is wedged and twisted into fissures in the rock from which, once it has hardened, it is difficult to remove. The eggs of catsharks, on the other hand (shown at right), are anchored to the branches of gorgonians with long spiral filaments that are attached to the tips of the eggs themselves, inside of which the young shark grows for eight or nine months, in most cases.

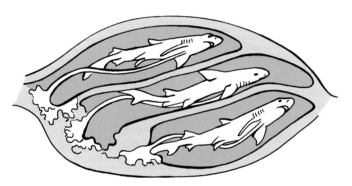

This illustration shows the uterus of a carcharhinid, containing three embryos. Although sharks are fish, they have evolved a system of reproduction very similar to that of mammals. This is especially true of the viviparous species, in which the young are nourished inside the body of the mother. In the ovoviviparous species, instead, nourishment is provided through a yolk sac.

embryo of ovoviviparous shark

vitelline sac

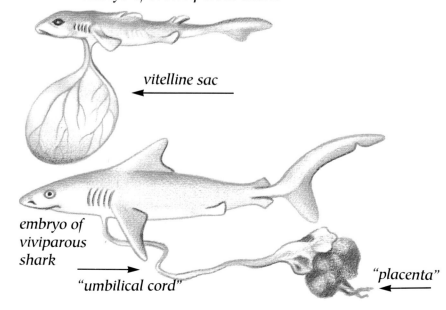

embryo of viviparous shark

"umbilical cord"

"placenta"

Hammerhead shark

Sphyrna spp.

Length: 90-500 cm

Distribution: temperate and tropical waters throughout the world

There are many species of hammerhead sharks, all of them marked by the bizarre head that widens out transversally. Aside from this distinctive feature, hammerheads resemble other sharks in terms of general body shape. The family Sphyrnidae is fairly recent, in evolutionary terms, and is rather homogeneous; what changes from one species to the next is, above all, the shape of the head, which, although it always tends to resemble a hammer, to some extent, ranges from the very elongated appendages of the *Eusphyra blochii* (which is certainly the most extreme of shapes) to the rather rounded lobes of the *Sphyrna tiburo* (which is known as the "bonnethead shark"). In sharp contrast with the general behavior of sharks, some species gather at times in huge groups, as happens in the Sea of Cortez. These sharks bear live offspring, and many species are migratory. Hammerheads are generally considered to be potentially dangerous to humans.

Why the "Hammer"?

A great many hypotheses have been advanced in an effort to explain why these sharks have evolved their strange, hammerlike heads. In fact, there is a lateral expansion of the orbital and nasal regions of the cranium, and the two lobes are supported by cartilaginous and connective tissue. The eyes are set at the two extremities. As for the possible function of the hammerhead, scientists have thus far considered two possibilities: that in some manner it helps to increase the shark's sensory capacities, or that in some way it provides improved hydrodynamic performance. These two hypotheses, of course, assume that the hammer shape is not simply a chance mutation that evolution "dragged along behind it."

The two protruding lobes of the head might represent a system that serves to increase the capacity for stereoscopic vision; indeed, the perception of a three-dimensional image requires two eyes set at a certain distance :from one

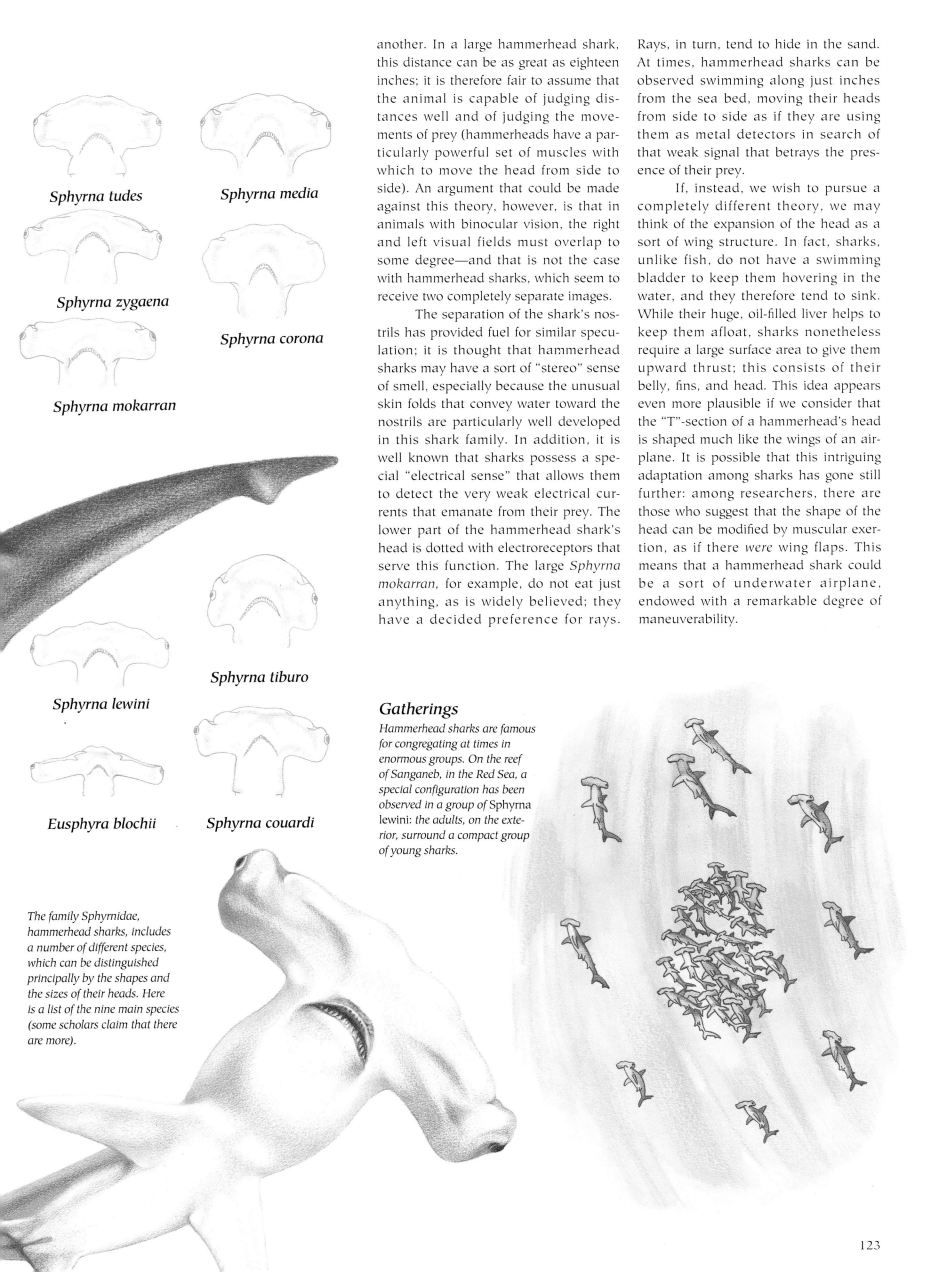

Sphyrna tudes

Sphyrna media

Sphyrna zygaena

Sphyrna corona

Sphyrna mokarran

Sphyrna tiburo

Sphyrna lewini

Eusphyra blochii

Sphyrna couardi

The family Sphyrnidae, hammerhead sharks, includes a number of different species, which can be distinguished principally by the shapes and the sizes of their heads. Here is a list of the nine main species (some scholars claim that there are more).

another. In a large hammerhead shark, this distance can be as great as eighteen inches; it is therefore fair to assume that the animal is capable of judging distances well and of judging the movements of prey (hammerheads have a particularly powerful set of muscles with which to move the head from side to side). An argument that could be made against this theory, however, is that in animals with binocular vision, the right and left visual fields must overlap to some degree—and that is not the case with hammerhead sharks, which seem to receive two completely separate images.

The separation of the shark's nostrils has provided fuel for similar speculation; it is thought that hammerhead sharks may have a sort of "stereo" sense of smell, especially because the unusual skin folds that convey water toward the nostrils are particularly well developed in this shark family. In addition, it is well known that sharks possess a special "electrical sense" that allows them to detect the very weak electrical currents that emanate from their prey. The lower part of the hammerhead shark's head is dotted with electroreceptors that serve this function. The large *Sphyrna mokarran*, for example, do not eat just anything, as is widely believed; they have a decided preference for rays.

Rays, in turn, tend to hide in the sand. At times, hammerhead sharks can be observed swimming along just inches from the sea bed, moving their heads from side to side as if they are using them as metal detectors in search of that weak signal that betrays the presence of their prey.

If, instead, we wish to pursue a completely different theory, we may think of the expansion of the head as a sort of wing structure. In fact, sharks, unlike fish, do not have a swimming bladder to keep them hovering in the water, and they therefore tend to sink. While their huge, oil-filled liver helps to keep them afloat, sharks nonetheless require a large surface area to give them upward thrust; this consists of their belly, fins, and head. This idea appears even more plausible if we consider that the "T"-section of a hammerhead's head is shaped much like the wings of an airplane. It is possible that this intriguing adaptation among sharks has gone still further: among researchers, there are those who suggest that the shape of the head can be modified by muscular exertion, as if there *were* wing flaps. This means that a hammerhead shark could be a sort of underwater airplane, endowed with a remarkable degree of maneuverability.

Gatherings

Hammerhead sharks are famous for congregating at times in enormous groups. On the reef of Sanganeb, in the Red Sea, a special configuration has been observed in a group of Sphyrna lewini: *the adults, on the exterior, surround a compact group of young sharks.*

Mako

Isurus oxyrinchus

Length: 180-250 cm

Distribution: warm and temperate
seas around the world

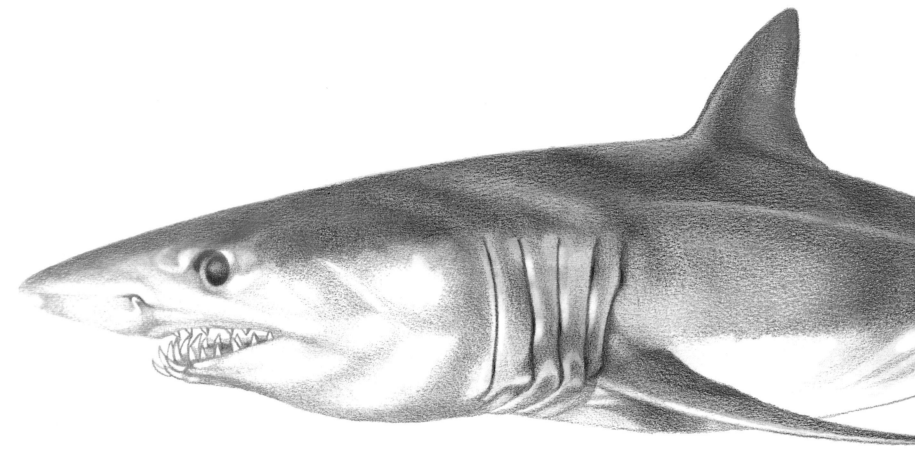

A member of the same family as the great
white shark, the mako is considered to be
the fastest shark in the world, since it can
move faster than fifty-five miles per hour.
The enormous efficiency of the mako's
muscles results from the fact that this
shark is capable of maintaining a body
temperature that is higher than that of its
environment, in much the same way that
warm-blooded animals do.

In the summer, the mako can be
found in relatively shallow waters, while
during the winter, it tends to shift to
deeper seas. It hunts large, fast fish such
as other sharks, tuna, and swordfish. A
very similar species is the *Isurus paucus*,
which is distinguished in particular by its
very long pectoral fins.

The mako is considered to be dangerous to humans, even though there is
very little documentation on mako
attacks. It is the shark that is most commonly hunted by sports fishermen; once
a mako takes the hook, it will fight stren-
uously and perform spectacular leaps
into the air. Moreover, mako makes for
particularly fine dining. The intensive
fishing to which the mako is currently
being subjected is causing some concern
that the species may be endangered.

Are Sharks Increasing or Diminishing in Numbers?

Australian diver Rodney Fox, survivor
of an attack by a great white, would
perhaps be the last person we'd expect
to worry about the fate of the sharks of
the world. Yet for a number of years,
he has been working actively to protect
the species to which his attacker
belongs. In fact, he believes that
sharks are endangered. Disappointing
was the experience of the Cousteau
Society which, in 1989, attempted to
film sharks for a documentary they
were making in southern Australia. In
the three weeks that the filmmakers
spent working on Dangerous Reef, they
managed to attract only three very
small white sharks, which did not even
dally for the time it took to get the
cameras into the water. Still, many
believe that sharks are in a phase of
dizzying and dangerous increase.
What is the truth? Are sharks growing
or declining in numbers?

It is difficult to give a simple
response, because no one knows for
certain how many sharks are swimming
in the oceans of the world. At times,
sharks seem surprisingly plentiful, as in
the case of the hammerhead sharks that
gather every year in enormous schools
in the Sea of Cortez (although this is a
phenomenon that is limited in scope).
Along the coasts of California, too,
sharks seem to be growing in numbers.
The reason might well be the increase
in the number of seals and otters since
1972, when the Marine Mammal Protection Act went into effect for the protection of sea-dwelling mammals; as a
direct result, the number of natural
predators preying on these mammals
has increased—specifically, the number
of larger varieties of sharks. In 1982,
fishermen of the Farallon Islands, near
San Francisco, captured in a single day
no fewer than four great white sharks.
The biologists who regularly observe
this area noted that the attacks on seals
and walruses diminished by half as a
consequence.

More wide-ranging considerations, however, might lead one to think that sharks are not having such a wonderful time of it after all. It is precisely their role as "great predators" that makes sharks so particularly vulnerable. As a rule, in fact, sharks are relatively rare—at least in comparison with their prey, the myriad small bony fish. Moreover, the reproductive "strategy" of many breeds of shark resembles that of many mammals; each individual lives for a relatively long time, growing and maturing slowly, and produces a comparatively small number of offspring, which come into the world fully formed and with a high chance of survival. This is in contrast to the fish that produce great numbers of eggs, of which only a few have any real chance of attaining maturity. In other words, the reproductive strategy of sharks calls for a very high investment in each individual, and therefore every loss has a greater and more harmful effect on the population as a whole.

Today, humans are the only true enemies of sharks, and this is demonstrated by one simple fact: off the California coast each year, from ten to twenty great white sharks die in fishing nets, while in the same area during the same period, only 0.13 humans die from shark attacks—roughly one every eight years. Aside from the accidental cap-

tures of sharks, one should take into account the deliberate ones: even though it has never become popular fare with the population at large, there is some demand now for shark meat, especially in Far Eastern markets ("shark fin" soup can be found on the menu of most Chinese restaurants). Then there are the sports fishermen: it would seem that the trickle-down effect of the movie "Jaws" has yielded more than its share of shark victims: for years afterward, great white sharks were slaughtered all over the world by every method imaginable, by shark hunters eager to imitate their Hollywood "heroes."

Some of the dangers of increasingly polluted seas—including the notorious rings of plastic used in industrial packaging—claim their share of shark victims. A shark that accidentally swims into one of these plastic rings cannot get free. Sharks have been captured that were horribly mutilated or deformed; as the sharks grow, the plastic cuts into their flesh and is absorbed by the tissues.

To conclude, there are certainly humans who would be happy to live in a world without sharks; there are others, however, who feel quite differently. In South Africa a law has been passed that is quite unprecedented—it protects great white sharks: since April 1991, it has been illegal to kill them in South African waters.

Positioned at the peak of a great many marine food chains, sharks are considered to be marine predators par excellence. This drawing demonstrates what happens in a number of species. The first step in the food chain, typical of every feeding network, is made up of plant forms. The microscopic algae of the phytoplankton transform inorganic materials into organic compounds and are the food upon which the zooplankton feed (tiny crustaceans, worms, coelenterates, etc.). In turn, the larger predators, such as mackerel, eat herring, and in turn are eaten by larger fish such as mako sharks. Herring are some of the mako's favorite prey, along with small tuna, codfish, and squid.

Great blue shark

Prionace glauca

Length: 180-240 cm

Distribution: temperate and tropical
   waters around the globe

Shark Repellent

The great blue shark, which may well be the most common of all requiem sharks (the Carcharhinidae family), can be easily distinguished by its particularly long and pointed pectoral fins. The snout is long as well and conical in shape. The eyes are large. The shark gets its name from the metallic blue coloration on its back. In general, blue sharks grow no longer than six feet, but there have been reports of individual specimens as long as twelve feet. They tend to prefer the open seas, although they are spotted off the coastline with fair frequency. They mostly eat fish and squid.

The blue shark is one of the sharks most likely to migrate great distances: specimens marked off the coasts of the United States, for example, have been found off the Spanish coast some time later. Often, blue sharks travel in same-gender groups. They are viviparous and are among the most prolific sharks; one female blue shark will produce as many as 25 to 50 young at a time, although the record for a single litter is 135 young. Many particularly aggressive divers like to swim with blue sharks after attracting them with bait. Although these sharks are potentially dangerous to humans, they are not particularly aggressive.

During World War II, the United States Navy supplied every sailor, along with the rest of his rescue gear, with "Shark Chaser"—a packet about six inches long and weighing about six ounces. This was the very latest development in the field of shark repellent, and if a sailor was shipwrecked and floating in the open seas, he was supposed to pour it into the water. The main ingredient of the packet was ammonium acetate, which exudes from putrefying shark meat. It was combined with a copper ion, resulting in copper acetate. Researchers chose this combination for its double-repellent action, which seemed to discourage sharks and cause them to lose their appetites. A black colorant had also been added, the chief purpose of which was to hide the potential victim from view.

It was not until after the war was over that it became painfully clear after more thorough testing that Shark Chaser had no value other than as a psychological crutch for terrified sailors. Unfortunately, it seems that most of the shark repellents that have been developed to date are equally useless. Despite this, efforts continue to develop an effective shark repellent capable of protecting shipwreck victims, scuba divers, swim-

mers, and waders. One method tried was that of a "curtain of bubbles," which involved a perforated tube lying under water on the sand with air being run through it under pressure. It was sold in Australia in the 1960s and proved useless even when tested against sharks in pools. This was not the only failed attempt at deterring sharks; an electrical wet suit that was supposed to ward off sharks with electrical jolts proved to be more unpleasant for the divers than for the predators. A black-and-white striped wet suit proved equally impractical; it had been designed on the theory that by resembling sea snakes, which are highly venomous, the scuba divers could enter the water without fear of attack.

Jacques Cousteau introduced the anti-shark club. This was a simple wooden bat tipped with a hooked nail, and with it scuba divers can push away intrusive sharks. It has often been effective, but the shark usually returns. The CO_2 dart is a gadget that injects carbon dioxide into the shark, swelling it up and forcing it to return quickly to the surface. But these darts, as well as the "bangsticks" loaded with bullets or even explosive charges, have proven to be extremely dangerous weapons, so much so that

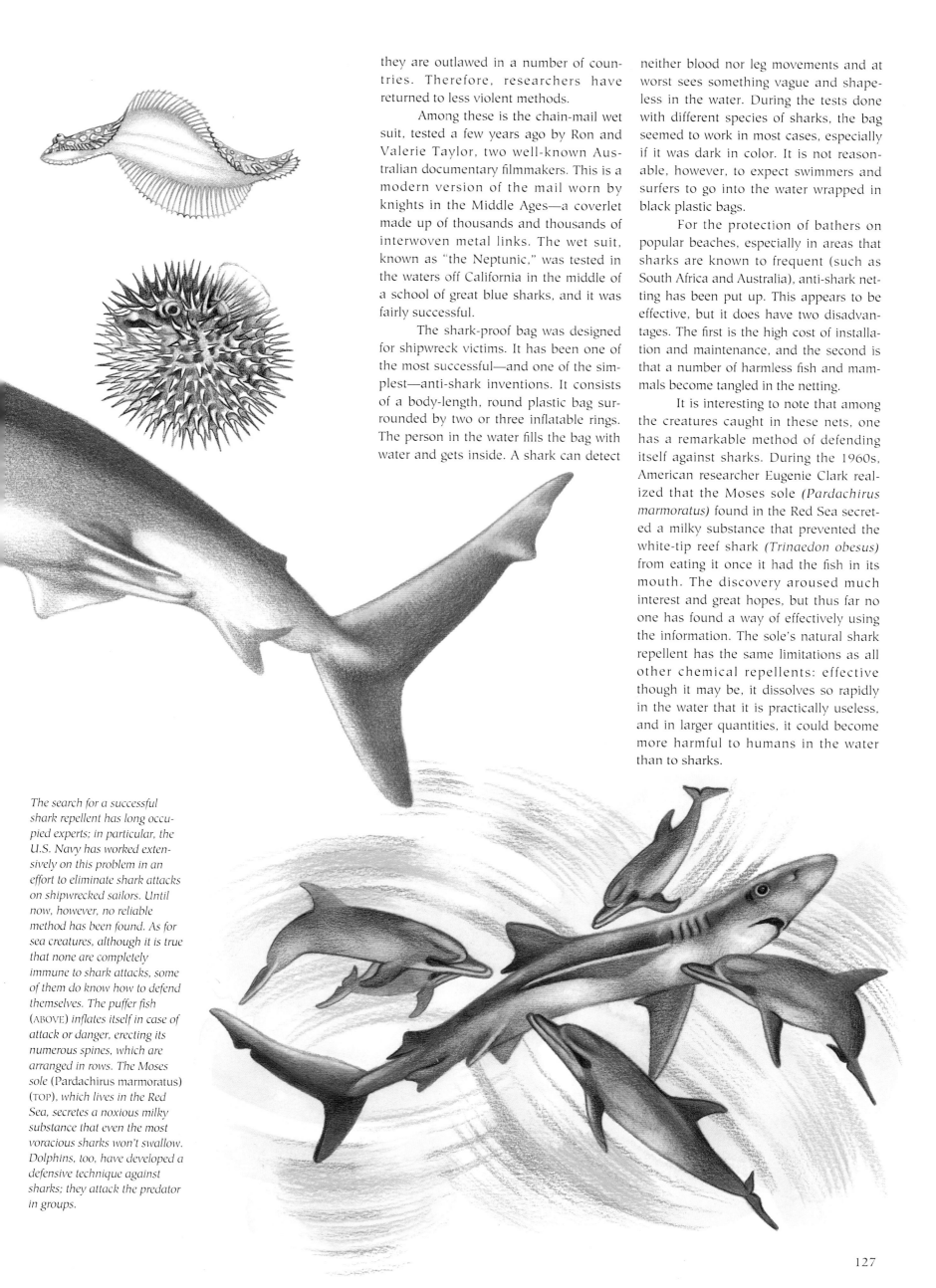

they are outlawed in a number of countries. Therefore, researchers have returned to less violent methods.

Among these is the chain-mail wet suit, tested a few years ago by Ron and Valerie Taylor, two well-known Australian documentary filmmakers. This is a modern version of the mail worn by knights in the Middle Ages—a coverlet made up of thousands and thousands of interwoven metal links. The wet suit, known as "the Neptunic," was tested in the waters off California in the middle of a school of great blue sharks, and it was fairly successful.

The shark-proof bag was designed for shipwreck victims. It has been one of the most successful—and one of the simplest—anti-shark inventions. It consists of a body-length, round plastic bag surrounded by two or three inflatable rings. The person in the water fills the bag with water and gets inside. A shark can detect neither blood nor leg movements and at worst sees something vague and shapeless in the water. During the tests done with different species of sharks, the bag seemed to work in most cases, especially if it was dark in color. It is not reasonable, however, to expect swimmers and surfers to go into the water wrapped in black plastic bags.

For the protection of bathers on popular beaches, especially in areas that sharks are known to frequent (such as South Africa and Australia), anti-shark netting has been put up. This appears to be effective, but it does have two disadvantages. The first is the high cost of installation and maintenance, and the second is that a number of harmless fish and mammals become tangled in the netting.

It is interesting to note that among the creatures caught in these nets, one has a remarkable method of defending itself against sharks. During the 1960s, American researcher Eugenie Clark realized that the Moses sole *(Pardachirus marmoratus)* found in the Red Sea secreted a milky substance that prevented the white-tip reef shark *(Trinaedon obesus)* from eating it once it had the fish in its mouth. The discovery aroused much interest and great hopes, but thus far no one has found a way of effectively using the information. The sole's natural shark repellent has the same limitations as all other chemical repellents: effective though it may be, it dissolves so rapidly in the water that it is practically useless, and in larger quantities, it could become more harmful to humans in the water than to sharks.

The search for a successful shark repellent has long occupied experts; in particular, the U.S. Navy has worked extensively on this problem in an effort to eliminate shark attacks on shipwrecked sailors. Until now, however, no reliable method has been found. As for sea creatures, although it is true that none are completely immune to shark attacks, some of them do know how to defend themselves. The puffer fish (ABOVE) inflates itself in case of attack or danger, erecting its numerous spines, which are arranged in rows. The Moses sole (Pardachirus marmoratus) (TOP), which lives in the Red Sea, secretes a noxious milky substance that even the most voracious sharks won't swallow. Dolphins, too, have developed a defensive technique against sharks; they attack the predator in groups.

Grey reef shark

Carcharhinus amblyrhynchos

Average Length: 180 cm

Distribution: Indo-Pacific

Are Sharks Intelligent?

Along with the white-tip reef shark and the black-tip reef shark, the grey reef shark is the most common shark found on the reefs of the Indo-Pacific region. It is often found in the areas where the reef and deeper waters meet. Elegant and streamlined like most of the requiem sharks, the grey reef shark has a characteristic black band along the lower section of the tail fin. It feeds on small fish, crustaceans, and cephalopods. This shark is a powerful swimmer, it tends to be active at night, and during the day it tends to gather with other sharks in small groups, often composed of younger sharks. It is therefore considered to be a moderately social animal. The grey reef shark is particularly inquisitive, and in areas where scuba divers are seen infrequently, it tends to approach newcomers, but then either disappears or keeps its distance. Although it is small and hunts small prey, it should be considered to be a threat to humans.

Sharks are often described as unpredictable. However, it's not quite that simple; a great deal of research has been done on the physiology of sharks, yet very little has been done regarding their behavior. And that should come as no surprise, since studying live sharks in the open ocean is not a simple proposition. In fact, very little is known about the behavior of sharks, and this field of research may well provide us with quite a few surprises.

A great many people think that sharks are big fish that are driven solely by hunger and therefore are completely "stupid." Others consider sharks to be doltish predators without any form of relationship with their fellow selachians. Indeed, a great many species, such as the large tiger sharks and the great whites, are solitary hunters. There is good reason for this: if too many of these huge predators were to operate in the same territory, they would probably soon go hungry.

But certain species of sharks are endowed with a surprising facility for communication. For instance, grey reef sharks at times launch full-fledged warnings to intruders: they swim along moving their bodies in an exaggerated fashion, such as in spirals, with their backs arched, heads raised, and pectoral fins depressed. When the earliest observations of this phenomenon were reported by scuba divers, some scientists did more thorough research into these warnings by intentionally provoking grey reef sharks. They found that the sharks' warnings seemed to be increasingly evident the faster and the more menacing the scuba diver's approach; the warnings also became more pronounced the more trapped the shark apparently felt by a situation, confirming that the action is actually a "warning"—followed, in some cases, by an attack.

This finding casts a new light on the behavior of sharks: if they warn something or someone, it means that they are not particularly interested in eating them; otherwise they would be more likely to attempt to surprise them. A ritual of threatening, on the other hand, is a type of communication among members of the same species, a behavior which may, on occasion, be extended to humans.

All of this suggests that sharks, or at least certain species, have some form of social interaction. And there are some distinctly "gregarious" sharks—perhaps the most spectacular demonstration is provided by the large gatherings of hammerhead sharks in the Sea of Cortez. There, hammerhead sharks gather by the hundreds, for reasons that remain completely unknown. The Sphyrna tiburo, a type of hammerhead shark that is well suited to captivity, was recently studied in aquarium conditions by researchers at the University of Miami. What they discovered was that not only is there a fairly complex and articulate form of communication among members of the same species, but there are even hierarchical relationships, which seem to follow considerations of size and gender.

If social interaction and certain mental capacities seem to go hand in hand, then one might well wonder whether sharks are intelligent. Some factors appear to favor one answer, and other factors favor another. As a general rule, animals that need to communicate among themselves must be endowed with a cer-tain mental elasticity; they cannot rely blindly upon instinct, and they must be able to learn. For this reason, for instance, orcas—large cetaceans that specialize in group hunting—spend a long period during their infancy in the company of their mother and other adults, from whom they learn everything they will need in order to survive. Such is not the case with sharks; they receive no parental care and employ no techniques of "coordinated" hunting.

However, one can hardly say that they are unable to learn; in captivity, many sharks have shown that they can rapidly adapt to new situations. By rewarding them with food, it is possible to teach them to respond to a certain sound or to distinguish between differently shaped objects. These are not outstanding performances—a great many other animals are capable of doing the same thing—but the "lessons" the sharks learn remain in their memories for a long time. And the fact that sharks have fairly long lives allows us to suppose that they may have time to learn a great many things in the undersea wilds. For example, there are sharks that have learned to associate the sound of an underwater rifle going off with the presence of prey, and upon detecting that particular sound, they regularly appear, even if no prey was hit.

At times, grey reef sharks assume a menacing stance, swimming in an especially "rigid" manner, with the back arched, the head turned upward, and fins pointing down. The illustrations below show (bottom) the "altered" swimming style and (top) the corresponding normal style. The fact that these sharks give their potential victims warning signals indicates that the attack is not necessarily part of a quest for food but may well be an attempt on the shark's part to defend its territory. In this case, then, the shark is not seeking out a direct confrontation with its enemy, but rather wishes to chase away the intruder through threats. The behavior of other sharks is different; the great white, for example, attacks suddenly, without the slightest warning.

Leopard shark

Triakis semifasciata

Average length, males: 140 cm

Average length, females: 170 cm

Distribution: northeastern Pacific

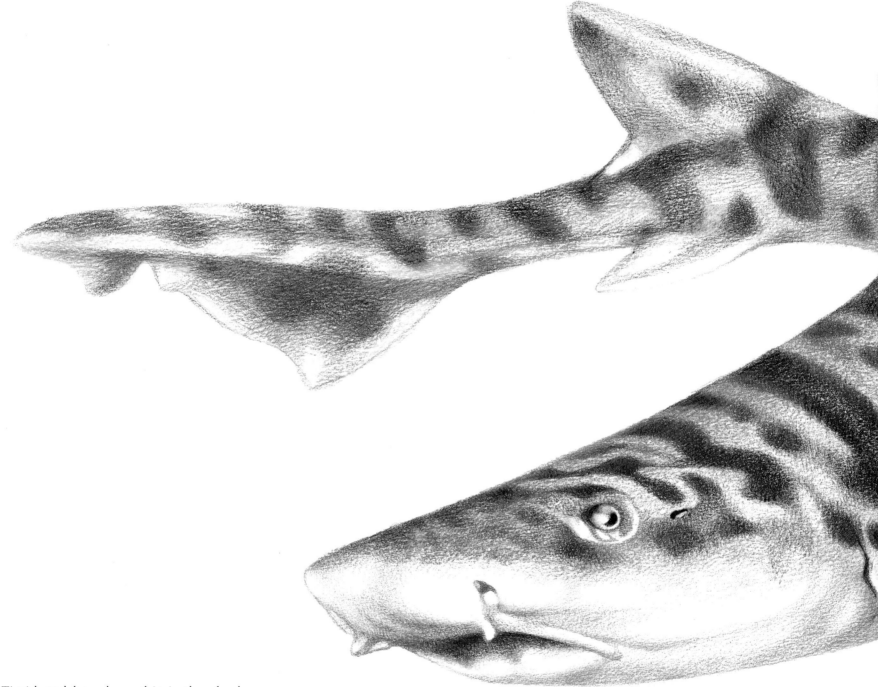

Timid and harmless, this is the shark most commonly seen in aquariums. Its distinctive coloration consists of a series of dark transversal stripes on its dorsal area, alternating with rounded spots, on a background that ranges from greyish-brown to silver. It is fond of shallow waters, and it can be found frequently along the Pacific coast from Oregon to the Gulf of California. It feeds on mollusks, crustaceans, bivalves, and small bottom-fish, and it often travels in large groups. Reproduction, which occurs frequently in captivity as well, is ovoviviparous. Females are considered mature when they attain a length of three feet, and after a year's gestation, they give birth to litters ranging from seven to thirty young.

Electrical Sense

Leopard sharks and other, similar small "aquarium" sharks, such as catsharks, have made it possible to discover the remarkable "electrical sense" of elasmobranches. Both sharks and rays possess a special sensitivity that allows them to detect extremely weak electric currents. This sensitivity is probably used in a number of different ways. The organs that perform this function were discovered some three centuries ago. They are called the "ampules of Lorenzini" (after the scholar who first described them, in 1678), and they form part of the complicated system of mechanoreceptors on the shark. In practical terms, this system is a series of

small bulbs set just beneath the skin and connected to the external environment of the shark through a channel filled with a gelatinous substance. The hundreds of small pores that can be seen on the head and on the snout of sharks and rays constitute the openings to the exterior of this system.

It was not until much more recent times that researchers were able to demonstrate that the ampules of Lorenzini are electrical sensors. A Dutch physiologist named Kalmijn demonstrated that certain members of the subclass Elasmobranchii possess the most acute electrical sensitivity in the entire animal world. He did this by recording the reactions of a ray (in particular, the variations in heartbeat) in response to extremely weak electrical stimuli. The surprising result was that the animal was capable of perceiving a tenth of a microvolt per centimeter (a microvolt is the millionth part of a volt). It remained to be seen, however, in exactly what way sharks and rays could make use of this remarkable capacity. It was believed that they used it to uncover and detect prey, and this hypothesis was confirmed through a series of experiments,

also conducted by Kalmijn, who used a starving catshark and a sole.

The sole, like many of the creatures upon which sharks normally prey, produces a relatively intense electrical field. The catshark demonstrated that it was immediately able to find the sole hiding under the sand. Above all, the shark was able to find the sole even when it was buried under the sand in a box made of agar; this gelatinous substance blocked visual, olfactory, and mechanical stimuli, but not electrical impulses. Clearly, the electrical field was sufficient for the small shark to find the place where the fish was hidden, yet the shark was completely unable to detect a dead sole placed in the same box. And the catshark could not detect even a live sole when it was hidden in a polyethylene box; this composite material insulates electrical fields. That is not all: the catshark would unleash its fury on an imaginary prey whenever an electrical field was created artificially under the sand using two electrodes.

Finally, a more elaborate version of this experiment was conducted in the ocean. A number of electrodes were arranged beneath an observation raft, along with a tube that released a slush of ground fish parts. The fish slush attracted sharks, which at first attempted to detect

the origin of the odor, but then, when the time came to attack, they went not for the tube but for the electrodes. Taking into account the fact that the power of a few microvolts of electrical field is completely lost at a distance of just a few centimeters, the scientists interpreted their data in the following manner: in all probability, sharks hunt at first by using their sense of smell and other senses, and only when they are at extremely close range, when they are already too close to see very well, do they use their electrical "sixth sense" as a final confirmation of the presence of their prey.

There is also a possibility that the sharks' electrical sense also helps them to orient themselves. In fact, an animal (which is conductive) that swims along in the earth's geomagnetic field in turn generates an electric field of its own, which varies in intensity according to the direction in which the animal is moving. During an experiment, a number of leopard sharks were placed in a tank with an artificial magnetic field; when the field was moved, they changed their direction of movement as well. And when, with the same system, the normal terrestrial magnetic field was neutralized, the sharks seemed disoriented, as if they had suddenly lost their "built-in compass."

Magnetic North   **Shark's direction**

Induced current

With particular emphasis on the leopard shark and catshark, a great deal of study has been devoted to the electrical sense of elasmobranches. This research, carried out by the Dutch scientist Kalmijn, involved experiments conducted in a tank, during which Kalmijn observed that the shark was successful in immediately finding a sole hidden beneath the sand, thanks

to its sensitivity to electrical fields. The shark, aided by its electrical sense, is capable of finding the sole even if the sole is hidden in a box that blocks all visual, chemical, and mechanical stimuli. When, on the other hand, the bait is formed of bits of dead fish, the shark can no longer depend upon its electrical sense and must therefore rely on its sense

of smell, searching in the general direction from which the odor originates. It has also been demonstrated that the shark cannot find a live sole hidden under the sand if the sole is electrically insulated. Lastly, the shark can be fooled by two electrodes hidden under the sand; when it perceives an electrical field, it believes that it comes from hidden prey.

Electrical receptors play an extremely important function in the life and survival of sharks. The ampules of Lorenzini, in fact, serve as a sort of internal geomagnetic compass, which is to say that sharks are, in all likelihood, capable of orienting themselves by detecting the earth's magnetic field.

Nurse shark

Ginglymostoma cirratum

Length: 2 to 3 meters

Distribution: Atlantic, Eastern Pacific

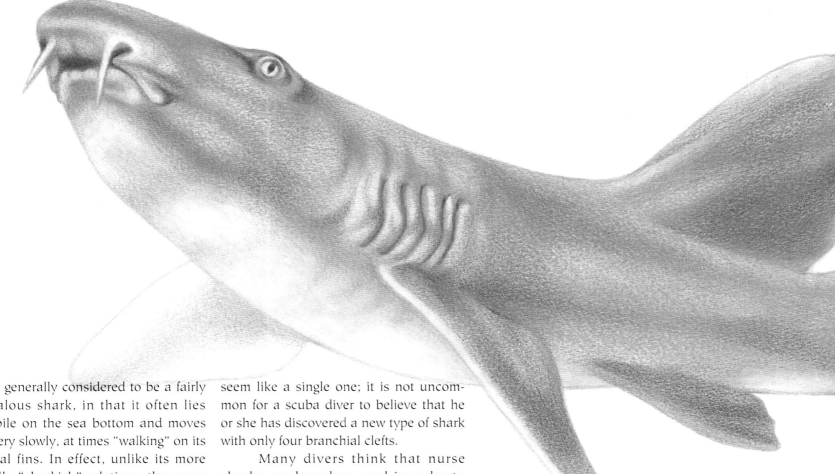

This is generally considered to be a fairly anomalous shark, in that it often lies immobile on the sea bottom and moves only very slowly, at times "walking" on its pectoral fins. In effect, unlike its more typically "sharkish" relatives, the nurse shark leads a sedentary life, spending it mostly searching for animals on the sea bottom and eating them, concentrating on shrimp, lobsters, sea urchins, and mollusks, and only occasionally going to the bother of catching a fish. Of the three or four species (the number is in dispute) that are considered to be nurse sharks, the best known is the *Ginglymostoma cirratum*, found frequently in tropical and subtropical seas. This shark can be found in the shallow waters off Florida and in the Caribbean, where it is particularly common.

Brown in color, it is easily recognized by the distinctive barbels on its snout, and by the absence of grooves around its nostrils. Adults are brownish in color, while younger nurse sharks are often covered with dark spots. The tail has virtually no lower lobe, while the upper lobe is quite large. The nurse shark has five branchial clefts, but the last two are at times so close together that they

seem like a single one; it is not uncommon for a scuba diver to believe that he or she has discovered a new type of shark with only four branchial clefts.

Many divers think that nurse sharks are harmless, and in order to rouse these sharks from their lethargy, they begin to needle them. Often, in such cases, the sharks react with sudden, unexpected, and well-placed bites. Although its teeth are small and best suited to breaking the shells of crustaceans and bivalves, a nurse shark is quite capable of lopping off a human finger.

Other, similar species are *Ginglymostoma brevicaudatum*, found in the waters off South Africa, *Ginglymostoma ferrugineum*, found in the Indo-Pacific, and *Nebrius concolor* of Australia. It is not clear how the term "nurse" came to be applied to these sharks. One possibility is that the name was taken from a nurse shark that was kept in an aquarium and "nursed"—fed artificially with fish pulp delivered through a tube.

Among the larger species, nurse sharks are those most often found in aquariums; the record for survival in captivity is held by one that survived for twenty-five years.

The Mystery of the "Sleeping" Sharks

Nurse sharks seem to favor underwater grottoes and often congregate in them in small groups; this is considered to be a distinctive trait of the species. Other sharks belonging to the family of the Carcharhinidae (the famed requiem sharks, which include species such as the great blue and the tiger shark) at times "sleep" inexplicably. This phenomenon has been observed in certain grottoes of the Yucatan Peninsula, where, in the 1970s, researchers ran into a group of *Carcharhinus springeri* inside a grotto, all of them so oddly lethargic and somnolent that they did not even react to the presence of the group of divers.

This behavior appeared to be quite paradoxical, if for no other reason than that sharks normally have to swim

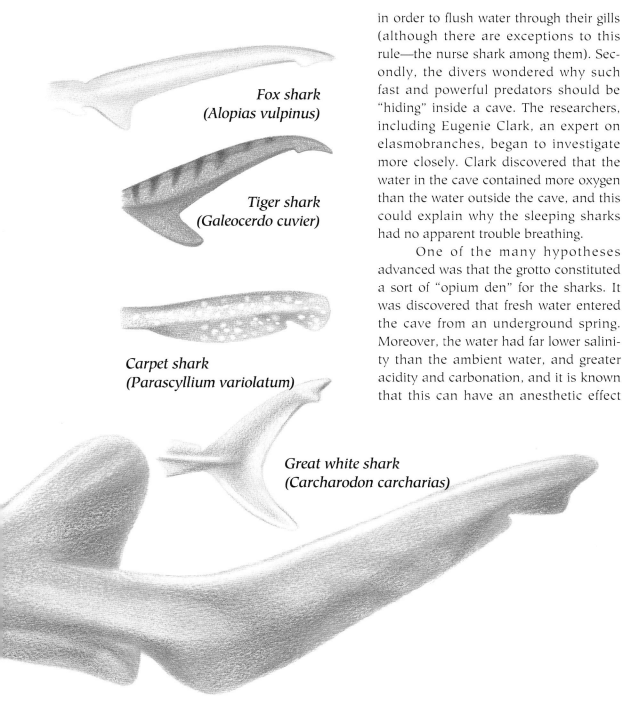

Fox shark
(Alopias vulpinus)

Tiger shark
(Galeocerdo cuvier)

Carpet shark
(Parascyllium variolatum)

Great white shark
(Carcharodon carcharias)

Cookie cutter shark
(Isistius brasiliensis)

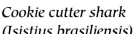

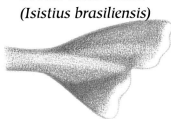

in order to flush water through their gills (although there are exceptions to this rule—the nurse shark among them). Secondly, the divers wondered why such fast and powerful predators should be "hiding" inside a cave. The researchers, including Eugenie Clark, an expert on elasmobranches, began to investigate more closely. Clark discovered that the water in the cave contained more oxygen than the water outside the cave, and this could explain why the sleeping sharks had no apparent trouble breathing.

One of the many hypotheses advanced was that the grotto constituted a sort of "opium den" for the sharks. It was discovered that fresh water entered the cave from an underground spring. Moreover, the water had far lower salinity than the ambient water, and greater acidity and carbonation, and it is known that this can have an anesthetic effect

on sharks. Another possible explanation was that the sharks were very sensitive to the electromagnetic fields created by the mixture of fresh and salt water, which could have had the same effect upon them that marijuana or alcohol has upon us. After observing the sharks of the Yucatan for a number of years, the scientists concluded that in reality the sharks were not sleeping at all, and their eyes actually appeared to be following everything that happened around them; they simply did not react as one might expect sharks to react. Perhaps what attracted them to the cave was the pleasurable sensation they felt there.

Another factor might well have been cleanliness. It is well known that many marine parasites release their grip upon fish when the salinity of the water changes, and there are marine species that visit the estuaries of rivers regularly for this very reason. A confirmation of this theory may come from certain sharks of the same species as the "sleepers"; they are far cleaner, without a sign of parasites, than their counterparts.

◄ The heterocercal tail, in which the upper lobe is more greatly developed than the lower lobe, is typical of most sharks and some bony fish as well.

In a grotto near the Yucatan Peninsula, groups of sharks of the genus Carcharbinus can be found motionless and apparently sleeping on the sea floor. The reasons for this behavior are not fully understood.
▼

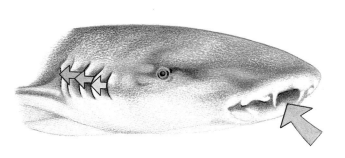

▲
As in all other species of fish, in sharks water enters through the mouth, is pushed through the gills, and emerges from the branchial clefts. In most species, there are five branchial clefts,

but some have six or seven. The gills, constituted by a series of cartilaginous arches with an intricate network of vessels, serve to convey the oxygen present in the water to the blood.

Basking shark

Cetorhinus maximus

Length: 8-10 meters

Distribution: cold and temperate
waters throughout the world

More than a few swimmers have been badly frightened by the sight of the classic and terrifying dorsal fin slicing through the water, followed by a hooked tail with a slightly larger upper section, and finally, a general silhouette not at all unlike that of the white shark, and monstrous as well—thirty feet long. Often, however, the shark in question is a basking shark—a toothless shark that may physically resemble the dreaded great white but does not prey on other animals and does not attack humans. It is a peaceful, harmless filter-feeder. As huge as it is docile, it is the only member of the family Cetorhinidae and probably leads a monotonous existence that consists largely of cruising through the ocean in search of plankton, gulping down huge quantities of small organisms floating in the water. For this reason, it often remains near the surface, where it

swims along slowly with its mouth open. Although it is quite powerful, and, when necessary, capable of violent movements, it often floats motionless in the water, with its dorsal fin, tail fins, and the tip of its snout breaking the surface.

Ranking just behind the whale shark in size, the basking shark is the second largest fish known to science. Unlike the whale shark, however, which prefers tropical waters, the basking shark lives in the cold and temperate seas of both hemispheres. In the Mediterranean, it makes its appearance primarily in the spring. Most distinctive are its five gill openings, which virtually encircle the head. Because of this, when the gills are open, they can give the odd impression that the head is about to fall off the rest of the body. Through the shark's open mouth, one can glimpse the interior of the branchial cavity.

In young basking sharks, the shape of the open mouth is quite distinctive: the upper section of the snout extends into a sort of small proboscis terminating in a fleshy tip, hooked slightly upwards: hence the name "elephant shark," as this fish is known in some parts of the world. In adult basking sharks, the profile becomes more regular, without the "beak," and therefore far more similar to the profile of other sharks.

The life cycle of the basking shark in many ways remains wrapped in mystery. Some information has come to us from the venerable fishermen of the North Atlantic, who have long fished the basking shark, chiefly for the oil in its liver. For instance, it would seem that there are far more females than males. Indeed, according to the fishermen, in order to capture a male one first had to

Young female head

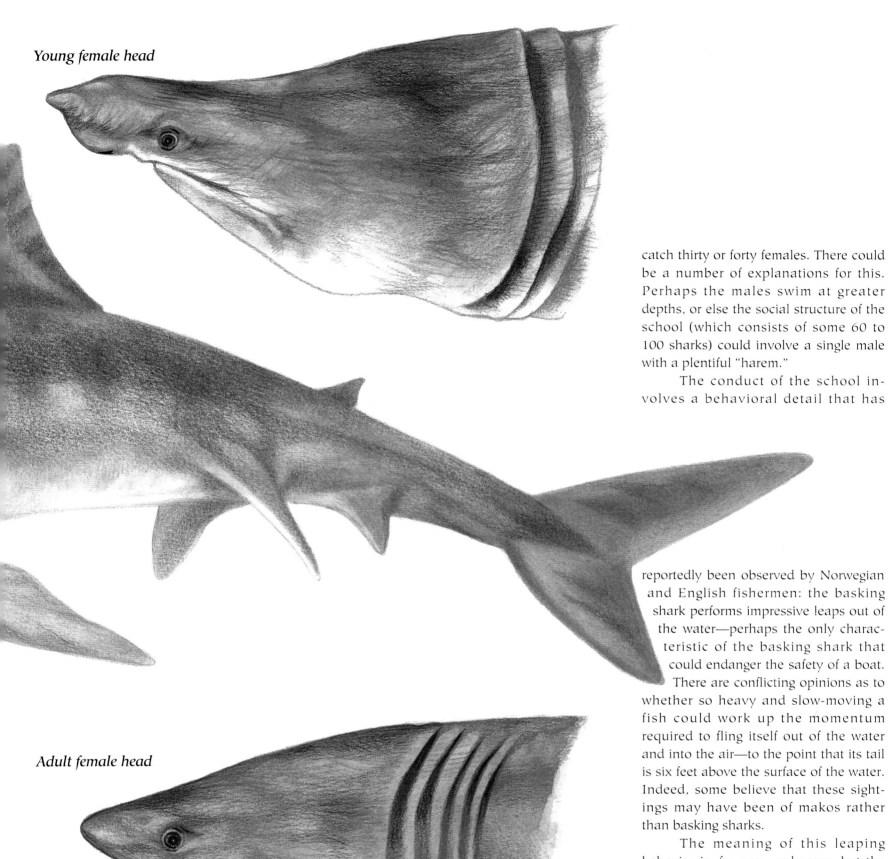

Adult female head

catch thirty or forty females. There could be a number of explanations for this. Perhaps the males swim at greater depths, or else the social structure of the school (which consists of some 60 to 100 sharks) could involve a single male with a plentiful "harem."

The conduct of the school involves a behavioral detail that has reportedly been observed by Norwegian and English fishermen: the basking shark performs impressive leaps out of the water—perhaps the only characteristic of the basking shark that could endanger the safety of a boat.

There are conflicting opinions as to whether so heavy and slow-moving a fish could work up the momentum required to fling itself out of the water and into the air—to the point that its tail is six feet above the surface of the water. Indeed, some believe that these sightings may have been of makos rather than basking sharks.

The meaning of this leaping behavior is, for now, unknown, but the very same hypotheses as are posited for leaping whales are offered to explain the behavior of the basking sharks: it may be a way of communicating with other basking sharks, or it may be a way of removing parasites from the skin. Speaking of whales, the basking shark was at first taken for a cetacean—until zoologists noticed that its tail was oriented vertically like that of a fish, and not horizontally, like those of whales and dolphins.

In a distinct variation from the norm in sharks, which usually keep in the same general form from birth to death, the snout of the basking shark varies greatly in shape according to the age of the shark: in the young shark, the snout is long and compressed with a fairly distinct tip at the upper extremity. The name "elephant shark" derives from the observation and description of the young of this species. In adult sharks, on the other hand, the snout is short, slightly conical, and rounded at the tip.

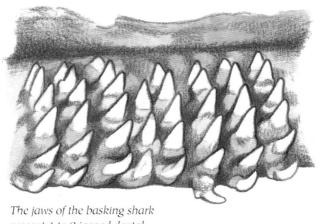

The jaws of the basking shark present 4 to 9 jagged dental rows, each with two hundred or more small conical teeth, made of dentine and enamel. Our limited knowledge about the biology of this species hinders us from determining the precise function of these teeth. They do not seem to be used in mastication, given the type of prey upon which the basking shark chiefly feeds, although we cannot rule out a more-or-less active role in feeding.

Eating and Breathing

No one has succeeded in providing an explanation as to why so close a relative of the mako and the great white should have, at some point in its evolution, abandoned the life of an ocean hunter and turned into a peaceful filter-feeder living on plankton. As a part of its adaptation to its specialization as a "grazer" in the world's oceans, this toothless shark has adopted a very special system of filter feeding that allows it to breathe and eat at the same time. Its gill openings are equipped with thousands of horny spines, or rakers, that serve to capture small organisms swimming in the water. When its mouth is open (and in an average adult male the open mouth covers an area of about a square yard), the basking shark can filter 1,000 to 1,800 tons of sea water in an hour when it is swimming through the soup of plankton at an average speed of two knots.

When the shark's mouth is open, powerful muscles cause the branchial rays to be erect. When the mouth is closed, certain elastic fibers cause the rays to collapse into a "folded" position, thus compressing inside the mouth the mucus and the food that have been collected.

These gill rakers are the source of a number of unanswered questions. The basking sharks that have beached themselves or have been captured during the cold season were completely devoid of rakers and were therefore incapable of procuring food. This fact is accompanied by the virtual disappearance of basking sharks during the winter months. Indeed, both in the Mediterranean and in the North Atlantic, the basking shark is often seen in the spring and in the summer, but rarely in the winter.

Many researchers are disposed to think that in the winter the basking shark stops eating and therefore stops swimming along on the surface and retires into what may not be a full-fledged state of hiberna-

The silhouette of the basking shark is distinguished by the pronounced "nose" as well as by branchial clefts that practically encircle the head. Basking sharks tend to swim in groups.

In the basking shark, gills are used not only in respiration, but also in the filtering of food. Small sea life, such as shrimp and plankton, are filtered by the branchial rakers, while the water flows on.

tion but a sort of dormant period in the deep. Most likely, it lies inactive on the sea bed awaiting the spring, positioned in such a way that the ocean currents provide a flow of water through its gills. In this phase, the old, atrophied branchial rays are shed and are replaced with new ones—as would be indicated by the vestigial rays developing under the skin of the basking sharks found in the winter. And if this is indeed what takes place, the basking shark is the only shark known to have a seasonal "shedding."

A 22-foot basking shark consumes no fewer than 600 calories per hour while swimming at its normal velocity of about two knots. In the summer, plankton is abundant and supplies energy at a greater level than the shark needs. In the winter, on the other hand, the plankton supply diminishes sharply, providing not more than 400 calories per hour. Therefore the basking shark, which must move constantly in order to eat, would not be able to consume enough to give it basic "operating" energy. It is therefore likely that the basking shark stocks up during the summer, converting the energy to fat, and then spends the winter resting. Whether this is what actually happens is not yet known, especially because in other regions, such as the waters off California, the basking shark is present year-round but is seen less frequently during the summer.

Are Basking Sharks Sea Serpents?

In 1808, on the shores of Stronsay in the Orkney Islands, a sea serpent washed up on the sand. Fifty-two feet in length, with six "paws" and the mane of a horse, it was classified as a new species—*H. pontoppidani.* It was a basking shark.

Decomposition of the body had played a nasty trick: indeed, when the body of a basking shark begins to decompose, the first parts to decay are the branchial arches, which "fall off," leaving only the cranium at the tip of a long and narrow body. The upper half of the tail fin also disappears and is no longer recognizable as such. As for the so-called "paws," these were probably the pectoral and pelvic fins and, in the case of a male, a set of claspers. And the "horse's mane" might very well have been the remains of the cartilage of the dorsal fin. The basking shark continued for many years to lend credence to the myth of the sea serpent.

These sharks do not always travel alone. For unknown reasons, at times two, three, or even more basking sharks will swim in single file, the snout of one immediately behind the tail of another. Swimming along with their fins cutting the surface, they can easily be taken for a single, lengthy, serpentlike animal.

Recorded Size of the Basking Shark

The average weight of an adult basking shark ranges from four to six tons. The liver can account for twenty percent of the shark's total body weight. One of the largest basking sharks ever recorded was forty feet long and weighed seventeen tons. It became entangled in fishing nets in Musquash Harbor, in the Bay of Fundy, in Canada, on August 6, 1851. An even larger basking shark was caught along the Norwegian coast at the turn of this century; it was forty-four feet long. The smallest basking shark ever caught was just under five feet long; it was probably a newborn.

The basking shark often swims on the surface, its mouth gaping open in order to swallow the largest possible volume of zooplankton. When its jaws are wide open, it is possible to *see clearly the branchial arches, upon which the respiratory plates and the branchial spines are situated; these are horny substances that are used in filtering food. During* *the winter, a period in which there is a shortage of food, the branchial rakers apparently fall off, and the basking shark remains at rest on the sea floor.*

Whale shark

Rhincodon typus

Length: up to 15 meters

Distribution: tropical areas
of all oceans

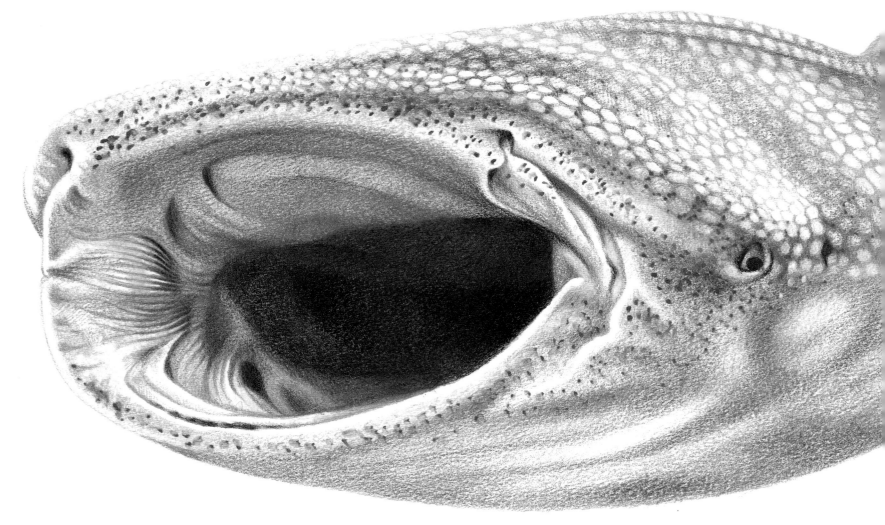

That the whale shark is classified as the only member of the family Rhincodontidae is accepted by most, but not all, biologists. Very little is known about whale sharks. Given that there is almost no money to be made from them, this species is rarely fished or hunted, and therefore it is studied even less. What is certainly true is that this fish is big: some whale sharks encountered at sea have been estimated at sixty feet, with a weight of up to twenty tons. This shark gets its name from its physical and other similarities to whales. Not only is the whale shark enormous in size, it is also a filter-feeder, taking plankton and other small prey from seawater.

In fact, the whale and the whale shark have independently developed very similar systems of filtration. Researchers are convinced that it is no accident that the largest creatures in the sea live by consuming huge quantities of tiny but extremely plentiful prey.

The whale shark lives on plankton and small fish, such as anchovies and sardines; the water enters the shark's mouth, which is remarkably wide—as much as six feet—and exits through the gills. The "filter," which serves to capture everything that is edible, is made up of a spongy material, a sort of very dense net with tiny openings, which is connected to the cartilage between one branchial arch and the next.

In the way that it feeds, the whale shark is very similar to the basking shark. There are, however, at least two major differences between the two. First, in the whale shark, the branchial clefts are shorter; second, the whale shark seems to eat more "actively": it opens its mouth before it meets the great banks of plankton, toward which it seems to steer intentionally, and it shifts from side to side so as to let nothing get away. The basking shark, on the other hand, does nothing more than swim in a more or less passive manner to and fro with its mouth wide open. Another indicator of the whale shark's "enterprising" approach could be an alternative technique it sometimes employs: at times it eats in a vertical position, pushing its head above the surface from time to time as if to take in the prey there as well.

Typically found in warm waters, whale sharks are distributed along an equatorial strip that extends from thirty degrees north latitude to thirty-five degrees south latitude, and only occasionally are they seen in temperate

The way that whale sharks reproduce is still a mystery. In fact, in 1953, when an egg containing a whale shark embryo was fished out of the waters of the Gulf of Mexico, it was thought that the species

must thus be oviparous. Nonetheless, many experts believe that the whale shark is ovoviviparous, which is to say that it keeps the eggs within its body until the moment they hatch.

The five branchial clefts of the whale shark are typical of many sharks, while the set of gill rakers that can be found inside the gills are similar to the whalebone of whales in terms of function.

waters or in warm currents such as the Gulf Stream. In particular, however, they favor those locations in which warm waters mingle with colder, plankton-rich currents. One of these areas lies between the Seychelles and the Mauritius Islands, where from time to time a whale shark has overturned a native craft. These incidents are not the result of any aggression on the part of the huge but harmless whales; they were most likely searching for plankton and didn't even notice the boats. In fact, whale sharks have always proven to be

extremely friendly to humans, and at times they have been so curious as to draw very near small boats and even have allowed themselves to be "ridden" by scuba divers. No one knows how many whale sharks there are in the world as of this writing, or whether their numbers are diminishing. Apparently they are quite rare, but it may simply be

that they spend long periods at great depths without returning to the surface.

Equally mysterious is the reproduction of whale sharks; it is not known whether this species deposits eggs or bears the developing eggs within the body of the mother. The true nature of things is difficult to discern because of two "discoveries" that are difficult to reconcile: on the one hand, female whale sharks have been captured that bore developing eggs in their bodies, and on the other hand, in 1955, an egg containing a whale shark embryo was fished out of the water.

Another unresolved question about whale sharks concerns the "camouflage" shadings on their backs. When viewed from above, the silhouette of the fish appears to be perfectly camouflaged to mimic the glitter of light on water. What is not known, however, is why it would be advantageous for a whale shark to camouflage itself, since it has no need to hide from prey or predator.

Shark Records

Though the whale shark does not attain the colossal size of the great blue whale, it still holds the title of the world's largest fish, followed by the basking shark. The smallest shark known to man is the dwarf dogshark, a deep-water shark from the Caribbean, which has been recorded at just under twenty centimeters in length at sexual maturity. The rarest shark is the megamouth. The fastest shark is the mako, which can attain speeds of up to fifty-five miles per hour. The most dangerous shark, for humans, is generally thought to be the great white. The shark with the largest documented number of offspring was a great blue that had 135 young in its womb when it was caught. At the other end of the spectrum, in terms of offspring, is the bull shark, which produces only two young at a time because of intrauterine cannibalism. Finally, two sharks are poisonous: the Greenland shark (*Somniosus microcephalus*), which is the only shark whose flesh is toxic if eaten, and the piked dogfish (*Squalus acanthias*), which has poisonous (but not lethal) spikes. (It should also be noted here that stingrays, which are "modified" sharks, are venomous and can inflict extremely painful injuries.) The piked dogfish, which is common in the waters of the Atlantic, is also considered to be the most common species in terms of absolute numbers.

Megamouth

Megachasma pelagios

Length: 4.5 meters

Distribution: unknown

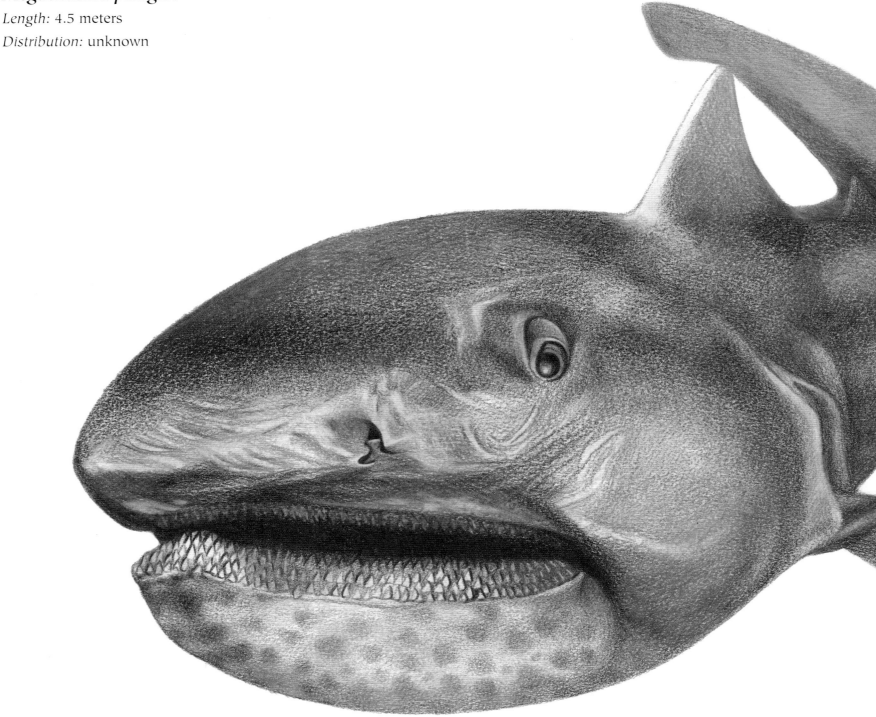

This shark is one of the more recent discoveries; to date only six of these sharks have been seen, almost all of them dead from becoming entangled in fishing nets. A live megamouth was seen off the California coast just a few years ago; it was filmed under water, and its movements were tracked by means of a radio homing device attached to its back. The information we have on megamouths is derived from a few individual specimens; while we know relatively little about its habits, behavior, and population biology, we do know something about its anatomy.

Like the whale and basking sharks, the megamouth is a filter-feeder. Unlike other sharks, the megamouth has a fairly soft body with loose flesh and very small,

flat dermal denticles. The shark's musculature is also unusually soft. All of this suggests (and the underwater films tend to confirm this) that the megamouth is a weak swimmer. The body of the megamouth is greyish black to dark blue, with a lighter color on the belly. The shark has broad pectoral fins and two dorsal fins, the first of which is larger. The tail flipper is markedly asymmetrical, the upper lobe being much more developed and flexible. But the shark's most distinctive characteristic is its huge mouth, with strange, rubbery "lips" and many rows of tiny teeth along the sides. Some parts of the mouth seem to be luminescent, perhaps in order to attract the small prey upon which this shark feeds.

It is believed that the megamouth

feeds by swimming along through shoals of plankton and gulping prey by suddenly opening its mouth, creating a negative pressure that sucks the prey in. Like those of other filtering sharks, the gills are equipped with a set of gill rakers, which capture the small particles of food. These sharks seem to populate the warm or temperate waters of the Indian and Pacific Oceans. It is not known how many there are in the world. Equally little is known about this shark's origins. The only clues available to paleontologists are a few fossil teeth dating from about twenty million years ago, discovered on the west coast of the United States, and others from forty to fifty million years ago, discovered in Argentina and England.

Do Sea Serpents Still Exist?

If, prior to November of 1976, someone had reported seeing a "monster" resembling the megamouth, few people would have believed it possible. Indeed, until that date no researchers anywhere had even the slightest hunch of the existence of a third filter-feeding shark. The first megamouth specimen known to science was captured accidentally by an American oceanographic ship off the island of Oahu, Hawaii. An enormous, unidentified fish had become entangled in one of the floating anchors. To the researchers who were given the megamouth's body, it constituted a truly remarkable discovery, and they had to create not only scientific names for a new genus and species, but even for a brand new taxonomic family.

One may well wonder, therefore, if there are other such "monsters" lurking under the waves. Indeed, many researchers feel quite sure that there are still a certain number of "sensational" species all over the globe just waiting to be discovered and classified, but especially in the oceans and seas, and especially among groups of large animals, such as sharks and marine mammals. Indeed, it is not necessarily true that the best "concealed" species are small animals; often the largest species are the last to be discovered. For instance, the whale shark was not described for the first time until 1828. Another example is the giant squid, the largest of all cephalopods, which was discovered in 1856.

There is an international organization that brings together respected scientists who are working to find "hidden" species—the Society of Cryptozoology, headquartered in Tucson, Arizona. Its members organize expeditions and gather reports of sightings, in search of certain types of animals whose existence is suspected but not yet confirmed, such as the celebrated Loch Ness monster, or Nessie's American counterpart, "Champ," who supposedly resides in Vermont's Lake Champlain.

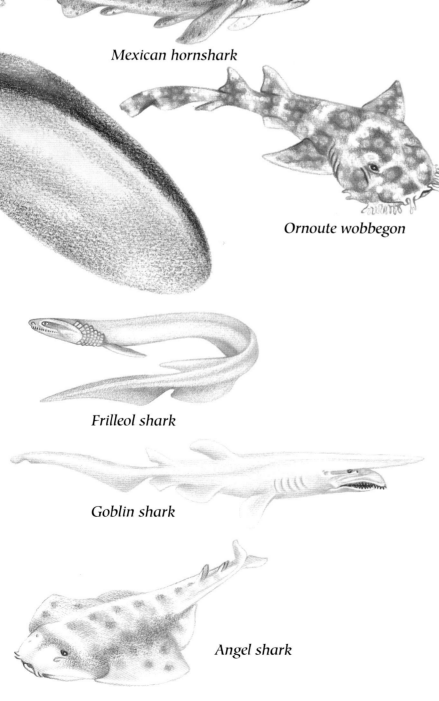

Megamouth

American saw shark

Port Jackson shark

Mexican hornshark

Ornoute wobbegon

Frilleol shark

Goblin shark

Angel shark

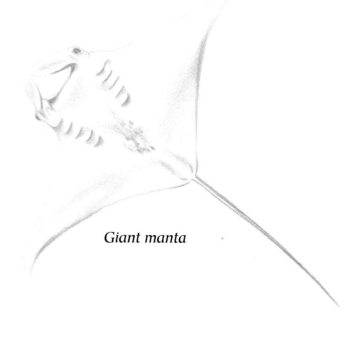

Giant manta

The megamouth is unquestionably one of the oddest-looking sharks there is; in reality, however, a great many of the megamouth's "relatives" have appearances that differ considerably from what is considered to be a "typical" shark. As for the manta ray (ABOVE), it is not technically a shark, but rather a close relative. Mantas belong to the order of rays, which are also cartilaginous fish, i.e., without bones. In the Mesozoic period, they were transformed and took on their current flat shape as a way of adapting to life on the sea bed. Though nearly all other rays continue to live on the sea bottom, lying on the sand, manta rays, through the course of evolution, returned to the environment of the open water, swimming freely, and grew to be considerably larger.

Shark Watching

Human beings who spend a great deal of time at sea usually fall into one of two categories—those who hope they will never meet up with a shark and those who will do anything to do just that. The latter group is much smaller than the former, to be sure, and it includes many scuba divers, a few of whom have doubtless been influenced by the movie and myth of *Jaws* and others who have a far more serious interest in these marine predators. If, until a few years ago, close encounters with sharks were the special province of underwater adventure-seekers, today what we might describe as "shark watching" seems to mirror a certain shift in our idea of what sharks are: they are not blood-thirsty monsters but splendid animals that have found the most appropriate way of adapting to their environment—animals that, for the most part, will do no harm if they are left alone. Of course, different species of sharks have different temperaments. It is quite one thing to find a gentle catshark, a carpet shark, or a leopard shark and quite another to encounter great whites, grey reef sharks, or hammerheads.

Aside from the need to take different precautions depending on the situation, at times the chief problem is finding the sharks that one wants to see, which can be far less simple than one might suppose. In many vacation spots, such as the Maldives or the Bahamas, scuba divers are regularly offered a dive with the sharks—usually grey reef sharks—though many of these "underwater circuses" have been closed because they are considered to be dangerous. Fish are fed to the sharks in order to attract them, and this often results in dangerous feeding frenzies. On the west coast of the United States, a number of specialized organizations offer encounters with great blue sharks, and during these encounters the people who sign on are lowered into the water in special protective cages.

Those who are looking for thrills and chills at all costs can go to visit the great white sharks off the coasts of Australia. From February to April, expeditions are organized from Port Lincoln, and the big predators are lured with bits of meat and other bait. If a great white shows up, the divers are lowered into the water in a strong protective cage.

Far more relaxing—but far more rare—is an encounter with a whale shark. Eugenie Clark, a researcher specializing in elasmobranches, recommends Ningaloo Reef off the west coast of Australia, where the big filter-feeding sharks seem to be most common in March and April, when the madrepores reproduce and the water is full of eggs. Both whale sharks and basking sharks can often be seen at the surface as they filter-feed just below. Off the Island of Mull, in the Hebrides, small daily expeditions that are organized during the summer often encounter basking sharks. In the Mediterranean, too, these sharks can be found from time to time, especially in the spring and early summer.

One of the most amazing shows put on by sharks is that of the huge assemblies of hammerhead sharks in the Sea of Cortez, where manta rays and whale sharks are often found as well. The hammerhead is a species that can be considered quite dangerous, but many shark-watching scuba divers who have had the good fortune of seeing as many as 100 or 200 at a time have encountered an unexpected problem: with the first breath they took, the noise of the rushing air bubbles from the breathing apparatus frightened the sharks away.

In the chart that follows, we show the habitats of a number of species as they have been counted along the coasts of North America from Canada to Mexico.

The cut-off between "high" and "low" sea floors is approximately 100 feet; this is done to show what depths are preferred by a given species of shark, independent of what habitat (surface or sea bed) it tends to haunt.

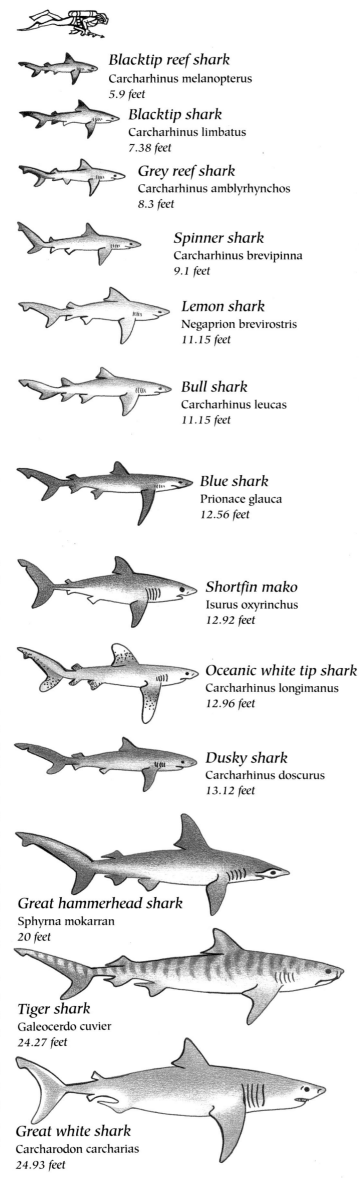

Blacktip reef shark
Carcharhinus melanopterus
5.9 feet

Blacktip shark
Carcharhinus limbatus
7.38 feet

Grey reef shark
Carcharhinus amblyrhynchos
8.3 feet

Spinner shark
Carcharhinus brevipinna
9.1 feet

Lemon shark
Negaprion brevirostris
11.15 feet

Bull shark
Carcharhinus leucas
11.15 feet

Blue shark
Prionace glauca
12.56 feet

Shortfin mako
Isurus oxyrinchus
12.92 feet

Oceanic white tip shark
Carcharhinus longimanus
12.96 feet

Dusky shark
Carcharhinus doscurus
13.12 feet

Great hammerhead shark
Sphyrna mokarran
20 feet

Tiger shark
Galeocerdo cuvier
24.27 feet

Great white shark
Carcharodon carcharias
24.93 feet